1.75

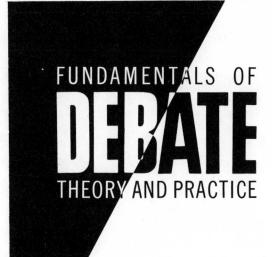

FUNDAMENTALS OF
DEBATE
THEORY AND PRACTICE

Otto F. Bauer

Bowling Green State University

SCOTT, FORESMAN AND COMPANY
Chicago   Atlanta   Dallas   Palo Alto   Fair Lawn, N.J.

PREFACE

Fundamentals of Debate: Theory and Practice is designed specifically for the high-school or college student who is interested in competitive debating. It provides brief, concise discussion of principles and ample opportunities for practical application of the principles.

Fundamentals of Debate: Theory and Practice can be used in at least three ways: (1) as a self-teaching source, when an instructor or debate coach expects a certain level of knowledge from his debaters; (2) as a textbook for courses in debate; and (3) as a supplement to argumentation textbooks, nine of which are cross-referenced in the appendix (see p. 126).

The book has a functional organization. The student begins with the basic principles that underlie educational debate. He then studies how to organize affirmative and negative cases, how to support his own case, how to attack his opponents' case and to defend his own, and how to compose and present debate speeches. Finally, he studies the methods of judging and evaluating debate contests.

Probably the most distinctive features of the book are its self-teaching aids. At the end of each chapter is (1) a programed test over the chapter; (2) an exercise that uses real life materials and experiences, with suggested answers in the appendix; (3) a list of assignments over the sample debate and for the proposition the student will be debating; and (4) a list of suggested references to professional journals in speech.

The author is grateful to the following people who read the manuscript and made many helpful suggestions: Douglas Ehninger and Michael M. Osborn of the State University of Iowa, and George W. Ziegelmueller of Wayne State University.

The author also wishes to acknowledge the help and inspiration of his former teachers and debate coaches, help that dates back to his first participation in interscholastic debate. He is indebted to Lorene Zenk of Sheridan Elementary School; to Homer H. Shelby of Elgin High School; to Professors Harold A. Brack of Drew Theological Seminary, Nicholas M. Cripe of Butler University, Joseph B. Laine of the University of Wisconsin, Oshkosh, and Glen E. Mills of Northwestern University.

Fundamentals of Debate: Theory and Practice is dedicated to Jeanette, Steven Mark, and Eric Paul.

Otto F. Bauer
Bowling Green, Ohio

CONTENTS

Basic Principles of Educational Debate

Educational debate, as we know it today, has developed over many years. It probably had its start with Protagoras of Abdera (481–411 B.C.), who is usually referred to as the "father of debate." Teaching in Athens, Sicily, and elsewhere, Protagoras selected topics on which his students argued both the pros and the cons, a practice that is the heart of present-day debate.

From medieval times until the mid-1700's, interest in debate was confined largely to the academic community. This is not surprising, because debates were commonly conducted in Latin in the form of syllogistic disputations and were concerned with abstruse points of theology or law. In such debates one disputant read a statement containing care-

2   fully worded syllogisms designed to support his side of the proposition, and then the other disputants refuted his arguments by offering counter-syllogisms.

When universities and student clubs began to sponsor debates in their own languages and to employ less formal logical patterns, interest in debate increased. In America the advent of intercollegiate debates in the late 1800's further stimulated this interest. The first intercollegiate debate probably took place in Evanston, Illinois, on November 29, 1872, when the Adelphic Society of Northwestern University debated the Athenaeum Society of Chicago University.[1] Today, thousands of high-school and college students each year receive instruction in argumentation and participate in educational debate.

To become an effective debater, you must, first of all, have a thorough understanding of such terms as *proposition, presumption, burden of proof, prima facie case, burden of rebuttal, probability, issues,* and *contentions.* You may never need to use most of these terms in an actual debate, but you must know the principles and concepts to which they refer, in order to meet the opportunities and the responsibilities which debate entails. You must also be thoroughly familiar with the major patterns and rules of modern educational debate. This chapter introduces you to these terms, patterns, and rules.

Obviously, there are various ways to define debate, but the following definition reminds us of the main features of debate:

Debate consists of opposing arguments on a given proposition between a supporting affirmative and an opposing negative.[2]

The proposition

As this definition makes clear, a debate centers on a *proposition* — that is, on a formally expressed judgment or opinion of a controversial nature ("Resolved: That the federal government should establish a national program of public work for the unemployed").

Propositions are of three kinds. The example just cited is called a *proposition of policy,* because it recommends a course of action or "policy" to be pursued in the future. A *proposition of fact* asserts that

1. Otto F. Bauer, "The Harvard-Yale Myth," *The AFA Register,* XI (Winter 1963), 20. The "Chicago University" referred to was opened in 1858 and closed in 1886.
2. James H. McBurney and Glen E. Mills, *Argumentation and Debate: Techniques of a Free Society,* Second Edition (New York, 1964), p. 4.

something is or is not so ("Joe Smith is guilty of armed robbery"; "Lack of recreational facilities contributes to juvenile delinquency"). A *proposition of value* asserts that something is good or bad, desirable or undesirable ("High excise taxes are detrimental to the American economy"; "Professor Brown is a good teacher").

Because most national debate questions involve propositions of policy, such propositions will be the primary concern of this book. The following two propositions of policy have been debated by colleges throughout the nation:

> Resolved: That the federal government should guarantee an opportunity for higher education to all qualified high-school graduates.

> Resolved: That the non-communist nations of the world should establish an economic community.

A correctly worded proposition for debate contains only one idea, an idea that is unambiguous in meaning and intent. Moreover, it gives the *presumption* to the negative team (the side which argues against the proposition; says "no" to the proposition) and gives the *burden of proof* to the affirmative team (the side which argues for the proposition; says "yes" to the proposition).

Presumption and burden of proof

In a debate on a proposition of policy, the presumption is with the *status quo* — that is, with "the way things are; the existing state of affairs." This does not mean that the present system is best, or even that it is widely accepted. It simply means that the system is in effect and will continue until someone succeeds in changing it. For example, we cannot assume that the Taft-Hartley Labor Act is the best labor law this country could have. But it is in effect, and anyone defending it would have the presumption because, unless it is repealed, it will continue to be "the existing state of affairs." A similar situation obtains with respect to a proposition of fact. When we say that a defendant is presumed to be innocent until proved guilty, we are not saying that he *is* innocent. He may very well be guilty, but, according to our laws, he cannot be declared guilty until sufficient evidence has been introduced to overcome his presumption of innocence.[3]

3. See Richard Whately, *Elements of Rhetoric* (London, 1828), Part I, Chapter 3, paragraph 2.

4   Because the affirmative side argues for changing "the existing state of affairs," it bears what is called the "burden of proof." In order to discharge this burden, it must demonstrate a sufficient cause for action by showing (1) that the present system has inherent shortcomings which the affirmative proposal will overcome, or (2) that the affirmative's proposal will bring about an improved state of affairs. For instance, a person who argues for compulsory arbitration of labor disputes must prove that present collective bargaining procedures are inadequate and that his proposal will correct the inadequacies, or that his proposal can assure labor-management relations which are significantly better than those now in effect.

Since the affirmative will lose if it cannot make a logical case for the rearrangement it desires, it has what is termed "the risk of the proposition" — that is, the risk of not being able to make good on the charges and proposals which it advances. This risk and the burden of proof which it entails remain with the affirmative throughout the debate and can never be shifted to the negative. If, however, the negative chooses not to defend the status quo, but rather to present an alternative proposal for solving existing problems (see Chapter 3, p. 39), it assumes an additional burden of proof to introduce evidence and argument sufficient to establish the superiority of its proposal. This obligation, which the negative assumes, does not alter the affirmative's original and continuing burden of proof; it merely asserts that any person who proposes to change the status quo must accept a burden of proof for his proposal.

Prima facie case

Since the affirmative bears the burden of proof, it must develop a *prima facie case* — that is, logical and convincing arguments for the proposal, ones strong enough to stand unless or until logical and convincing arguments are introduced against it. If the affirmative does not create a prima facie case — does not develop a statement capable in its own right of justifying a change to the proposed new system — it loses the debate by default, because this is the least that can be expected of persons who advocate a new state of affairs. If, however, the affirmative does present a prima facie case, it overcomes the presumption of the negative, at least temporarily. To re-establish its presumption, the negative then must present a *prima facie rejoinder,* in the form of objections strong enough to overcome the affirmative's charges. Such a rejoinder, in turn, bestirs the affirm-

ative to new action in an effort to repair and advance its case. And so
the debate proceeds, with each side alternately entering evidence and
argument for or against the proposition.

Burden of rebuttal

Although the burden of proof always rests with the affirmative, a
burden of rebuttal shifts back and forth between the two sides as each
presents arguments worthy of answers. The burden of rebuttal is the
obligation to engage not only in refutation, which is the destruction
of opposing proofs, but also in defense of one's own case against an
opponent's attack. Proper assumption of the burden of rebuttal by
both the affirmative and the negative assures the give-and-take of
controversy, the essence of debate.

Probability

Probability, which is the quality of being likely, is an important
concept in debate. Oftentimes a debater will assert categorically that
he has *proved* a contention. In reality, however, no one can establish
certainty in the realm of human beliefs and actions, and assuredly
not when these permit of enough doubt to be controversial. No
matter how much information or knowledge one has, he cannot say
exactly what caused a given war or depression, how *all* men feel or
react under certain circumstances, or what *precisely* the effects of a
particular policy will be. People simply are too diverse in their habits
and values, and human affairs are too complex and variable to permit
any such absolute statements.

But while you are not expected to present *absolute* proofs (evidence
and reasoning), you are expected to establish the strong probability
or likelihood of your contentions. To do this, you must discover and
present the best possible proofs to support your contentions. In
criminal law, a defendant is judged guilty only if the evidence
presented shows that he is guilty beyond a reasonable doubt. In
educational debate, the greater the degree of probability you can
establish, the more likely you will be to get your position on the
proposition accepted. For example, while affirmative debaters are not
required to show that their proposition *will* be adopted, they cannot
hope to convince many people of its worth unless they at least can
show both that it *should* and it *could* be—that it is, indeed, a good
proposal which is within the realm of practical possibility.

6   *Issues*

You must be able to recognize the *issues* in a dispute. Issues are *vital* and *inherent* questions upon whose answers the acceptance or rejection of the proposition hinges. They always should be phrased in such a way that the affirmative answers "yes" to them, and the negative answers "no." In the proposition "Resolved: That the federal government should establish a national program of public work for the unemployed," some of the issues would be: Is the problem of unemployment sufficiently serious to require federal action? Are existing measures incapable of solving the problem? Would a national program of public work best solve the problem? Is the federal government the best agency to undertake the solution? Would a program of public work not only reduce unemployment but also produce other benefits?

Issues are *vital*, because the affirmative's failure to secure a "yes" answer to any one of them means the loss of the debate. And issues are *inherent*, because they arise out of the clash between the proposition and the denial which is entered against it. If a question is not vital and inherent, it is not an issue.

Let us examine the proposition "Resolved: That the Communist Party of America should be outlawed." Assuming that the negative denies this proposition directly — says that the Communist Party of America should *not* be outlawed — one of the issues would be, "Is the Communist Party a threat to the United States?" This issue is vital, because if the Party is not a threat, there is no need to outlaw it. And it is inherent, because it arises out of the clash produced when the proposition advanced by the affirmative is denied by the negative. (If, for instance, instead of answering as it did, the negative had said, "The outlawing of any political party is against our constitutional principles," this issue would not have arisen.)

Stock issues

In debating a proposition of policy, many debaters organize their cases around *stock issues* — questions which are so fundamental that they arise whenever a new policy is discussed:

1. Is there a need for a change?
2. Would the proposal of the affirmative meet the need?
3. Would it produce benefits rather than harmful results?

These issues (often referred to as *need, plan,* and *benefits*) arise in part from the relationship between the burden of proof and the presumption. Because the affirmative bears the burden of proof, it must present a statement that justifies a change from the present system and also warrants the adoption of the particular policy which it proposes. In terms of the stock issues, in addition to showing a *need* for a change, the affirmative must show that the specific *plan* which it advocates would meet the need, and that the plan would produce *benefits* rather than harmful results. That each of these tasks is vital to the successful establishment of the affirmative's case is obvious, for no reasonable man would wish to adopt a proposal if it were *unneeded* or *impracticable,* or if it would bring *new evils.*

If you analyze a proposition of policy in terms of the stock issues, you usually will discover the other issues which a dispute entails. For example, apply the first stock issue — Is there a need for a change? — to the proposition "Resolved: That the Communist Party of America should be outlawed." In searching for arguments to justify outlawing the Communist Party, you probably would discover these two issues: Is the Communist Party of America a threat to the United States? If so, are our present laws not strong enough to meet this threat? These questions — both aspects of "need" — are issues, because if the affirmative is unable to present a logical and convincing case for a "yes" answer to both, it clearly will fail in its effort to establish a need for a change.

Contentions

Both affirmative and negative debaters support their position on the issues by means of statements known as *contentions.* Students sometimes confuse issues and contentions. To see the difference, let us look at the proposition "Resolved: That the federal government should establish a national program of public work for the unemployed." One of the issues would be: Is the problem of unemployment sufficiently serious to warrant federal action? To justify their "yes" position on this issue, the affirmative debaters might offer such contentions as these: Unemployment is extremely high despite the general prosperity of our country. It will become greater unless some federal action is taken. The fact that thousands of people cannot get employment is responsible for the alarming increase in crime. The affirmative debaters, of course, would have to support these contentions with evidence and reasoning. Note that the debaters

8   could lose a contention and still win the debate, but because the issue, as distinguished from the contentions, is vital to the life of the proposition, they could not lose the issue—or any of the other issues—and still win.

An examination of the 1960 presidential campaign should further clarify the relationship between issues and contentions. The proposition debated was: "Resolved: That John F. Kennedy and not Richard M. Nixon should be elected President of the United States."[4] There were at least two issues: (1) Does the nation's state of affairs warrant a change in our national, Republican leadership? (2) Can John F. Kennedy solve the problems better than Richard M. Nixon? In attempting to convince the voters that "yes" was the correct answer to the first issue, Mr. Kennedy contended that there were serious faults in the Republican administration's handling of (a) our foreign policy, (b) our preparation for defense, (c) our economic policy at home, and (d) other aspects of our nation's state of affairs. Obviously, Mr. Kennedy could lose some of these contentions, but he could not, in theory, win the decision if he lost the issue: Does the nation's state of affairs warrant a change in our national, Republican leadership? Nor could he win the decision if he lost the second issue—the vital, inherent question of whether he could solve existing problems better than Mr. Nixon.

Educational debate procedures

There are various kinds of debate, and they function under various rules and procedures. Both legislative debate and judicial courtroom debate have strict rules. Political debate, on the other hand, has few regulations, and these are usually limited to the regulations governing elections and to the laws pertaining to libel and slander. In adherence to established rules and procedures, educational debate most resembles legislative and judicial courtroom debate.

Ordinarily, in present-day educational debate, two persons form an affirmative team, which agrees to support the proposition for the duration of the debate. Similarly, two persons form a negative team, which agrees to oppose the proposition for the duration of the debate.

4. Other ways of phrasing the proposition are possible, but this phrasing emphasizes the Presidency, places the burden of proof on Mr. Kennedy, and presents Mr. Nixon as the defender of the current administration, and thus gives him the presumption.

Constructive and rebuttal speeches. Both sides make constructive and rebuttal speeches. During the constructive speeches, each side presents its case and the supporting evidence and reasoning.

During the rebuttal speeches, each side tries to refute the case of its opponents and to defend or rebuild its own case. Obviously, the negative will include a great deal of refutation in its constructive speeches, and the affirmative will include defense of its case in its constructive speeches. Each side, moreover, should refrain from altering its case in its rebuttal speeches. In other words, rebuttal speeches should be used for attack against and for defense of arguments that have already been presented in the constructive speeches.

Speaking order and time limits. The following pattern is the one most widely used for speaking order and time limits:

Constructive speeches	*Time*
First affirmative	10 minutes
First negative	10 minutes
Second affirmative	10 minutes
Second negative	10 minutes

Rebuttal speeches	*Time*
First negative	5 minutes
First affirmative	5 minutes
Second negative	5 minutes
Second affirmative	5 minutes

In *cross-examination debating* (see pp. 82–84), each team is permitted to question the opposing team on the proposition. Such debating usually follows a scheme like this:

Constructive and cross-examination speeches	*Time*
First affirmative constructive	8 minutes
Second negative questions first affirmative	4 minutes

First negative constructive	8 minutes
First affirmative questions first negative	4 minutes
Second affirmative constructive	8 minutes
First negative questions second affirmative	4 minutes
Second negative constructive	8 minutes
Second affirmative questions second negative	4 minutes

Rebuttal speeches	*Time*
Negative (either speaker)	5 minutes
Affirmative (either speaker)	5 minutes

• When you have a clear understanding of the basic principles and general procedures of debate, you will be ready to study the organization of affirmative and negative cases, the subject matter of the following two chapters. To test your understanding of the principles and concepts discussed in this chapter, work through the following programed test and the exercise. To help you further in understanding the debate process, prepare the assignments and read one or more of the references on page 15.

Programed test

1. First question: If the affirmative has presented a sufficient cause for action, it has presented a prima facie case.
    If you think this statement is true, go to item 13.
    If you think this statement is false, go to item 10.
2. Correct. You have completed the programed test for Chapter 1.
3. The statement is not true, because absolute certainty is virtually impossible in areas that involve human events. The debater must, though, establish strong probability.
    Return to item 11.
4. The statement is not true, because the burden of proof always remains with the affirmative. The negative, however, assumes an *additional* burden of proof if it advocates any changes in the status quo.
    Return to item 10.

5. Correct. Next question: The affirmative can lose an issue, but, theoretically, it cannot lose a single contention.

If true, go to item 12.

If false, go to item 15.

6. The statement is not true, because the negative, not the affirmative, supports "things as they are." The affirmative *must* advocate a significant change from the present system.

Return to item 17.

7. The statement is true. Debaters should not make changes in their basic positions or points of view during the rebuttal speeches. Such changes would demonstrate the weakness of the original case.

Return to item 15.

8. Correct. Next question: The presumption rests with the negative.

If true, go to item 17.

If false, go to item 14.

9. Correct. Next question: Both sides have the burden of rebuttal.

If true, go to item 11.

If false, go to item 16.

10. Correct. Next question: The burden of proof shifts back and forth from affirmative to negative.

If true, go to item 4.

If false, go to item 8.

11. Correct. Next question: A debater must establish absolute certainty for his arguments.

If true, go to item 3.

If false, go to item 5.

12. The statement is not true, because all issues are vital. The affirmative can lose a contention and still win the debate, but it cannot lose a single issue.

Return to item 5.

13. The statement is not true, because a prima facie case not only must present a cause for action but also must establish the desirability and practicability of the proposed action.

Return to item 1.

14. The statement is true. The presumption cannot rest with the affirmative under any circumstances, because the affirmative is advocating a change from the status quo.

Return to item 8.

15. Correct. Next question: Rebuttal speeches are for attack against and for defense of arguments presented in the constructive speeches.

If true, go to item 2.

If false, go to item 7.

16. The statement is true, because each side has the obligation to reply to arguments that are worthy of an answer. In rebuttal, each side must defend its own position against its opponents' attack and must refute its opponents' arguments.

Return to item 9.

17. Correct. Next question: One way to describe the burden of proof is to say that the affirmative supports "things as they are."

If true, go to item 6.

If false, go to item 9.

Exercise

Read the following excerpts from a debate⁵ between Harold E. Stassen and Thomas E. Dewey. Write out your answers to the questions given after the excerpts. After you have written out your answers, check them against the suggested answers in Appendix D, page 127

Harold E. Stassen:

I journeyed to many of the European countries and to Russia and questioned leaders of many nations. . . .

I have reached the conclusion that the Communist organizations in the world are absolutely directed by the rulers of Russia. . . . that the objectives of these Communist organizations in the world are to overthrow free governments, to destroy the liberties of men, and to bring other countries under the domination of the dictators of Russia. . . .

I do not think it is generally realized in America that we do not have any law to effectively oppose the actions of these Communist organizations, either overground or underground. . . .

A law has been introduced known as the Mundt-Nixon bill, which provides that it shall be unlawful to attempt in any manner to establish in the United States a totalitarian dictatorship, the direction and control of which is to be vested in . . . any foreign government. . . .

5. The debate took place over the radio from Portland, Oregon, on May 17, 1948. Stassen, former governor of Minnesota, and Dewey, then governor of New York, were candidates for the Republican presidential nomination. The statements are excerpts from the constructive speeches. The entire debate can be read in *Vital Speeches of the Day*, Vol. XIV (June 1, 1948).

Now, the chairman and secretary of the Communist Party of America have protested that this bill would outlaw their organization. I agree that it would and I say that it should. . . .

There seems to have been some mistaken idea that the Communists were outlawed in Russia. This is not correct. . . .

Another mistaken impression is the claim that if we outlaw the Communist organization, we thereby endanger the liberties and civil rights of other people. This is not true. In Canada the party was outlawed for years and the people lost none of their liberties. . . .

I submit that the Communist organization in America . . . should be outlawed.

Thomas E. Dewey:

He [Mr. Stassen] asked me . . . :

1. Do you agree that the Communist organizations in the world today are under the direction of the Kremlin in Moscow? Certainly.

2. Do you agree that the world Communist organization is a threat to world peace? Certainly. . . .

. . . My interest is in preserving this country from being destroyed by the development of an underground organization which would grow so closely in strength, were it outlawed, that it might easily destroy our country. . . .

. . . He says he is for the Mundt bill because, says Mr. Stassen, it outlaws the Communist Party. . . .

Here's what Mr. Mundt says on May 14, 1948: "This bill does not outlaw the Communist party." . . .

Now, this outlawing idea is not new . . . .

The fact is that the czars of Russia were the first people in the world to follow this idea. . . .

. . . Mussolini outlawed Communism, and they grew and flourished underground. . . .

. . . I am unalterably . . . against any scheme to write laws outlawing people because of their religious, political, or social or economic ideas.

I am against it because it is a violation of the Constitution of the United States and of the Bill of Rights. . . .

There is an American way to do this job. . . . We have now twenty-seven laws on the books . . . outlawing every conceivable act of subversion against the United States. . . . This . . . expedient of outlawing . . . failed in Canada. . . . they tried it once

14   and the Communist party grew so powerful and dangerous that
they repealed the law. . . .

1. State the proposition being debated.

2. What kind of proposition is it?

3. Who has the burden of proof?

4. Who has the presumption?

5. What are the issues?

6. Was a prima facie case presented? Explain.

Assignments

For the sample debate in Appendix A:
1. Read the entire debate in order to get a general impression of the
   format of an interscholastic debate.[6]
2. In what ways were the principles of debate referred to by the
   speakers?

6. See Appendix B for a list of sources of other sample debates.

3. Describe the major issues discussed in the debate.
4. Was a prima facie case presented by the affirmative? Explain.

For the proposition you will be debating:
1. What kind of proposition is it? Explain.
2. Evaluate the strength of the negative presumption.
3. Describe the relationships of the stock issues to the proposition.

Suggested references[7]

Baird, A. Craig. "The College Debater: 1955," *The Southern Speech Journal,* XX (Spring 1955), 204–211.

Ehninger, Douglas. "Debating as Critical Deliberation," *The Southern Speech Journal,* XXIV (Fall 1958), 22–30.

Miller, Gerald R. "Questions of Fact and Value: Another Look," *The Southern Speech Journal,* XXVIII (Winter 1962), 116–122.

Newman, Robert P. "Analysis and Issues—A Study of Doctrine," *Central States Speech Journal,* XIII (Autumn 1961), 43–54.

Nobles, W. Scott. "Symposium: Tournament Debating and Rhetoric," *Western Speech,* XXII (Fall 1958), 206–210.

Robinson, James L. "III. Are We 'Overlegalizing' School Debate?" *The Speech Teacher,* IX (March 1960), 109–115.

Terris, Walter F. "The Classification of the Argumentative Proposition," *Quarterly Journal of Speech,* XLIX (October 1963), 266–273.

7. All references are to articles appearing in *The Speech Teacher, Speech Monographs, Quarterly Journal of Speech, Central States Speech Journal, The Southern Speech Journal, Western Speech, Today's Speech,* and *The AFA Register,* called *The Journal of the American Forensic Association* since January 1964.

CHAPTER
TWO

Organizing the Affirmative Case

Defining the terms in the proposition
Studying the proposition
The traditional case
Sample affirmative case
The comparative-advantage case

The affirmative debaters, to overcome the presumption of the negative, must present a prima facie case, that is, a case justifying a change from the present system to the system described in their proposal. In the following pages, two types of affirmative cases are discussed—the traditional case and the comparative-advantage case. Because the traditional case is commonly used by debaters and generally adaptable to most propositions of policy, it is treated more fully.

Defining the terms in the proposition

The first affirmative speaker always has the responsibility, at the beginning of the debate, of defining any ambiguous terms in the proposition. Such definitions enable both sides to be sure that they are talking about the same things. As a matter of fact, your first step in case analysis should be to seek an understanding of the terms in the proposition. Many terms have generally accepted meanings and require no definition; others may require clarification or limitation. Look for a moment at the proposition quoted in Chapter 1: "Resolved: That the federal government should guarantee an opportunity for higher education to all qualified high-school graduates." The meaning of *federal government* would certainly not have to be explained. But what about *higher education?* Should this be taken to include commercial trade schools as well as colleges and universities? And in this context, how exactly should *guarantee* and *qualified* be defined? The first affirmative speaker, of course, should provide reasonable definitions; if the definitions *are* reasonable, the negative should accept them, and the rest of the debate should be conducted on the basis of those definitions.

Studying the proposition

To construct a good case, you must learn as much as you can about the proposition. This means reading widely in many sources, discussing the proposition with experts, and making on-the-spot observations when such first-hand research is possible and advisable. Methods of research are discussed in Chapter 4.

After you have studied the proposition carefully and have thought about it a great deal, you are ready to begin to formulate your case.

The traditional case

The traditional case is organized around the stock issues:

1. Is there a need for a change?
2. Would the affirmative proposal meet this need?
3. Would the proposal produce benefits rather than harmful results?

With this organization, you first try to demonstrate that there is a *need* for a change from the present system; second, you describe your proposal or *plan;* and, finally, you explain how your plan not only will correct the evils of the present system but also will produce additional *benefits*.

18   *Organizing the need—the first stock issue.* In developing the cause for action (the need for a change), you should not be content merely to list the evils in the present system. You should make your indictment reflect one or more of the various kinds of reasoning, and you should support your reasoning with sound evidence.[1] This combination of reasoning and evidence provides proof for the affirmative position on the first stock issue of need.

Of the different types of reasoning, both *sign* and *causal* reasoning are appropriate and effective in establishing a need for a change. Reasoning from sign establishes the *existence* of a problem, and reasoning from cause shows *why* the problem exists.

Suppose you as a member of the affirmative team were supporting a proposal for federal world government. To establish a need for a change from the present system, you might first contend that the present system (each of the nations of the world with unlimited sovereignty) is unsatisfactory, and, to support your contention, you might cite many instances (or signs) of tensions and conflicts throughout the world. In so arguing, you would be reasoning from sign—you would be using these various instances to prove that serious problems existed.

You might further contend that the tensions and conflicts were *caused* by the unlimited sovereignty of each nation (a basic feature of the present system or status quo). If you could cite sufficient evidence to establish the causal connection between unlimited national sovereignty and the existing tensions and conflicts, you would have a strong, *inherent* indictment of the present system; you would be demonstrating that the tensions and conflicts were an inseparable part of the present system. Of course, superficial problems or ones that could be solved without basic changes would not constitute an inherent indictment of the present system.

The first part of the affirmative case, using sign and causal reasoning, can be structured in the following manner:

I. There is need for a change, for

Sign   A. Serious problems are present in the status quo, for
reasoning   1. Example (sign of problem)
            2. Example (sign of problem)
            3. Example (sign of problem)

1. Evidence and reasoning are discussed in Chapter 4.

Causal
reasoning

B. These problems are caused by certain basic characteristics of the present system, for
1. Characteristic 1 causes these problems.
   a. Evidence
   b. Evidence
2. Characteristic 2 causes these problems.
   a. Evidence
   b. Evidence
3. Characteristic 3 causes these problems.
   a. Evidence
   b. Evidence

Remember that you must discover *inherent* flaws in the present system in order to establish a need for a change to an entirely new order. Many affirmative teams had difficulty discovering inherent flaws in the current system when the national debate proposition advocated compulsory health insurance. One team, however, successfully used sign and causal reasoning to establish a need for a change. First they contended that there were serious faults in the current system by pointing to the various groups of people—notably the low-income families and the chronically ill—who were excluded from health insurance under the current voluntary plan. They then contended that the profit motive, a basic characteristic of the current system, would prevent these people from ever being eligible for health insurance. The affirmative thus prepared the way for the discussion of their plan—a government program of compulsory health insurance—which would, according to their contention, correct what they considered to be the inherent faults of the current plan.

Organizing the plan—the second stock issue. Remember that the affirmative must present a prima facie case, and that a prima facie case not only justifies a change from the present system *but also shows that the change should be to the specific plan advocated by the affirmative.*

Obviously, the length at which the plan will be explained depends upon the proposition under debate. For example, consider the following two propositions: "Resolved: That Red China should be admitted into the United Nations," and "Resolved: That the non-communist nations of the world should establish an economic community." The plan for the first proposition could be stated briefly, but the plan for the second would probably require careful, detailed explanation.

20 Some plans may be familiar to the audience and so require a minimum of description; others may be quite new and revolutionary and so demand a great deal of explanation. Whatever the length of your plan, describe it as specifically, concisely, and clearly as possible. Organize the details (even of a long plan) under no more than three or four main categories. A complicated plan with many main divisions may confuse you as well as your opponents and the audience. Select the main categories and hold to them throughout the debate. For example, you might organize the details of your plan under these main headings: Structure, Function, and Method of Enforcement. The second part, then, of the affirmative case, the discussion of the plan, could be outlined in this way:

II. The affirmative proposes the following plan to solve the problems cited in the present system:
   A. Its structure will consist of . . . .
   B. It will function in the following manner . . . .
   C. Its method of enforcement will be . . . .

Organizing the benefits—the third stock issue. In developing your answer to the third stock issue—Would the proposal produce benefits rather than bring harmful results?—you must detail the expected effects of the proposal. At this point the case shifts from analysis and description to *prediction.* Obviously, if you are to predict accurately—if you are to develop the benefits contention successfully—you need to know what constitutes a good prediction. Why should a listener accept your predictions as probable and accurate? Do you have any evidence to support your prediction? What authorities would be most reliable? The following questions and comments should clarify the elements behind a good prediction—reliable evidence and sound reasoning. The first two questions are concerned with the reliability of authorities (the sources of evidence), and the second two deal with appropriate patterns of reasoning.

1. *How close is the cited authority to the situation?* An experienced social worker who has devoted many years to working with juvenile gangs should be a fairly good judge of the kind of program the members of these gangs would accept and benefit from— a better judge, say, than a legislator who had had no experience with juvenile delinquents.
2. *What degree of control does the cited authority have over the situation?* A powerful union leader can predict with great accuracy

when his union will begin its strike, for he has a high degree of control over union activities.

3. *To what extent are variable factors recognized and accounted for?* Many families predict their expenditures for the year, but their budget may be unrealistic if they do not provide for possible variations in taxes, food costs, and other expenses.

4. *Is there historical precedent?* Has the plan been successful in other situations, or has the predicted occurrence happened before? If so, the probability of its being successful again or of its happening again is increased.

These questions and comments suggest that the best evidence a team can use to support a prediction is a judgment or opinion of an authority who is close to the situation or one who has a high degree of control over it. And the best kind of reasoning a team can use to support a prediction is reasoning that recognizes and accounts for significant variable factors.

In developing this third part of the affirmative case, you should discuss two basic kinds of benefits: (1) those that correct the "evils" in the present system, and (2) the additional benefits that might accrue. Do not underestimate the importance of actually listing the benefits to be expected from your proposal. Give each one emphasis by treating it as a separate point. And do not forget to present evidence that your benefits actually will occur. Remember that evidence is especially important in making an accurate prediction.

Some affirmative debaters make the mistake of devoting more time to refuting the evils the negative alleges will be produced by the proposition than to developing the advantages of their proposal. If you present and support significant advantages, your defense against the negative's alleged evils will be more effective. Moreover, you will provide your listeners with a sound base for comparison.

The third part of the affirmative's case, the benefits issue, may be outlined in the following manner:

III. Many benefits will result from the affirmative plan, for
    A. The plan will correct the evils cited in the present system, for
        1. Evil #1 is corrected, for
           a. Evidence
           b. Evidence
        2. Evil #2 is corrected, for

      a. Evidence
      b. Evidence
   B. The plan will have additional benefits, for
     1. It will have _____ benefit, for
      a. Evidence
      b. Evidence
     2. It will have _____ benefit, for
      a. Evidence
      b. Evidence

Presenting the case. As you recall (see Chapter 1, p. 9), each debater usually is allowed ten minutes for his constructive speech. In presenting the case described in the preceding pages, your team could organize its efforts in various ways. The following outline suggests one satisfactory distribution of responsibilities and time:

First affirmative	*Time*
1. Introduction to problem and definition of terms	2 minutes
2. Need issue	7 minutes
3. Summary and conclusion	1 minute

Second affirmative	
1. Description of plan	2 minutes
2. Benefits issue	2 minutes
3. Defense against negative arguments and rebuilding of need issue	5 minutes
4. Summary and conclusion	1 minute

As an alternative arrangement, the second affirmative could rebuild the affirmative's need arguments first, and then present the affirmative's plan and benefits. Depending upon the time requirements of your case, you may wish to present the plan in the first constructive speech.

If you organize your need, plan, and benefits in the manner described, you should have a sound case structure; however, you have not created a logical statement for a change until you have provided supporting evidence. Chapter 4 will suggest ways of supporting your case, and Chapter 5 will consider ways of testing evidence and reasoning. You should subject your own case as well as the case of the opposition to these tests.

Sample affirmative case

The following skeleton case is based upon arguments presented by Adlai E. Stevenson in various speeches, written reports, and news conferences during the 1956 presidential campaign. His basic arguments have been adapted to the pattern of the traditional affirmative case. The sample negative case, which appears in the next chapter, is Dwight D. Eisenhower's response to Stevenson's arguments.

Resolved: That the United States should stop testing the hydrogen bomb.

  I. There is a need for a change in our testing policy, for
    A. Serious problems exist, for
       1. Fall-out from nuclear tests is dangerous to mankind, and
       2. A stalemate exists in negotiations on disarmament.
    B. Present testing policies cause the above problems, for
       1. There is unlimited testing, and
       2. Even small gains in disarmament are prevented.
 II. The affirmative proposes the following plan:
    A. The U.S. will stop testing H-bombs.
    B. The Soviet Union will be challenged to curtail its testing.
    C. Enforcement will be accomplished by a built-in inspection system.
III. Many benefits will result from the affirmative plan, for
    A. The plan will correct the problems cited in the present system, for
       1. Radioactive fall-out will be sharply reduced, and
       2. The stalemate in disarmament negotiations will be broken.
    B. The plan will have additional benefits, for
       1. Initiating this policy will be a cold war victory, and
       2. Military strength will be maintained, for
          a. Research in nuclear weapons would continue, and
          b. Testing of delivery systems would continue, and
          c. Testing of smaller nuclear devices would continue.

Sometimes affirmative debaters decide upon a comparative-advantage case. With such a case they usually begin by agreeing with the negative that the status quo has no drastic faults. They claim, however, that the affirmative proposal offers more advantages or benefits than are offered by the present system. Because of this "comparative-advantage," they urge the adoption of the affirmative proposition.

You should not use the comparative-advantage case as a way of circumventing the need argument. If you perceive serious faults in the present system, you should indict those faults and seek to correct them. On the other hand, it should be clear that a properly formulated comparative-advantage case, like the properly formulated traditional case, is a prima facie case; if substantial advantages can be achieved from a new proposal, it is logical to change from the present system to that proposal.

Conditions which necessitate the comparative-advantage case. If the present system is generally sound and without glaring faults, how can you justify a change? If a person owns a new Ford convertible in excellent condition, why should he consider buying a new Cadillac convertible? Are there serious shortcomings in the performance of his Ford? What arguments can the Cadillac dealer use? He probably would claim better performance and greater comfort, along with more prestige. But all of these arguments are only greater advantages; he has not offered a serious indictment of the Ford's performance or comfort. His only real argument is that the Cadillac is "better."

If you cannot point to serious faults in the status quo, you will have to argue that your proposal can do a "better" job, and that, comparatively speaking, more advantages are likely to accrue from your proposal than from the present system. You also might argue that problems may arise which only your proposal is likely to solve. For example, assume that qualified high-school students who apply for college scholarships have little difficulty today in acquiring them. How could you as a member of the affirmative team argue for a national scholarship program? You might sensibly predict several situations for which the presently available scholarships would not provide—for example, the likelihood that businessmen's demands for employees with college educations will force more students to apply for the available scholarships; the likelihood that most scholarships, which are ordinarily for set sums, will soon be inadequate to provide for the rising costs of college tuitions, books, and living expenses in general; the likelihood, with the present rate of population growth, that the numbers of qualified high-school graduates will be greatly increased in a few years. Further, you could argue that your program would do a "better" job of providing scholarships and that certain advantages are more likely to accrue from a national program than from many independent sources of aid.

Essential nature of the comparative-advantage case. If you argue that the affirmative proposal will produce certain benefits that the present system cannot achieve, you are looking into the future, making a prediction. Although you are not indicting the present system as a whole, you are indicting significant omissions within it. If you suggest a future problem which the present system is not likely to resolve, you are predicting an occurrence, predicting that the present system cannot cope successfully with it, and predicting that your proposal can. Note that while the benefits contention of the traditional case is built upon prediction, virtually the entire comparative-advantage case is built upon prediction. For this reason, debaters using the comparative-advantage case should be particularly careful to use the tests of a good prediction, as they formulate their case (see pp. 20–21).

Organizing the comparative-advantage case. There are at least two basic ways of organizing the comparative-advantage case. Using the first pattern, which ordinarily is the more effective, you would begin by showing that the absence of certain qualities in the present system is a cause for action. You would then demonstrate that this lack in the present system would probably prevent the attainment of certain benefits and the solution of certain problems likely to occur in the future. And, finally, you would point out how the affirmative proposal would produce the benefits and would solve the future problems.

In using this first pattern, you might organize your efforts in the following way:

First affirmative	*Time*
1. Introduction to problem and definition of terms	2 minutes

    2. Absence of qualities or
       prediction of problems
       in the present
       system
    3. Summary and conclusion

Second affirmative

1. Description of plan	2 minutes
2. Benefits issue	2 minutes
3. Defense against negative arguments and rebuilding of first affirmative's arguments	5 minutes
4. Summary and conclusion	1 minute

Using the second pattern, you would make no attempt, at the outset, to establish a cause for action. Instead, you would first describe the present system and the affirmative proposal, and, in the process, make clear the differences between them. Then, you would present the benefits to be derived from the affirmative proposal, discussing them in detail and providing sound support. The main value of this pattern is that it provides for a more detailed presentation of the benefits, the only possible cause for action.

If you follow this second pattern, you might organize your efforts in this way:

First affirmative	*Time*
1. Introduction to problem and definition of terms	2 minutes
2. Description of present system	3 minutes
3. Description of affirmative proposal	4 minutes
4. Summary and conclusion	1 minute

Second affirmative

1. Benefits issue	4 minutes
2. Defense against negative arguments and rebuilding of first affirmative's analysis	5 minutes
3. Summary and conclusion	1 minute

In each of these two patterns, the second affirmative could begin with a rebuilding of the first affirmative's analysis and arguments, if this arrangement seemed appropriate.

• The affirmative has the challenge of creating and presenting a prima facie case. The negative has an equal challenge of subjecting that case to careful analysis and presenting a case strong enough to defeat the affirmative proposition. Effective negative cases will be the concern of the following chapter.

Programed test

1. First question: The traditional affirmative case is ordinarily the most logical one to use, because the status quo commonly has short-comings.
   If true, go to item 13.
   If false, go to item 17.
2. The statement is not true, because many terms have commonly accepted meanings. It would be a waste of important time to define such terms.
   Return to item 13.
3. Correct. Next question: A comparative-advantage case based solely on a better plan of action is prima facie.
   If true, go to item 16.
   If false, go to item 12.
4. The statement is not true, because closeness to a situation normally means a person is better informed, and impartiality should not be sought at the expense of knowledge. Determine the extent of partiality after you are assured of sufficient knowledge.
   Return to item 16.
5. The statement is not false. A plan should have adequate detail, but it should not become complicated in its use of detail; the audience should not be confused by the plan.
   Return to item 15.
6. Correct. You have completed the programed test for Chapter 2.
7. Correct. Next question: Reasoning from cause establishes the existence of a problem, and reasoning from sign shows why the problem exists.
   If true, go to item 11.
   If false, go to item 15.

28   8.   The statement is not true, because "significant need arguments" would indicate that a traditional affirmative case would be more logical. If significant shortcomings exist, it is logical to try to correct them.

Return to item 10.

9.   Correct. Next question: The traditional affirmative case emphasizes prediction in answering the third stock issue.

If true, go to item 10.

If false, go to item 14.

10. Correct. Next question: Affirmative debaters should use the comparative-advantage case to concentrate on a plan of action and to minimize significant need arguments.

If true, go to item 8.

If false, go to item 3.

11. The statement is not true, because the reasoning patterns should be interchanged. "Sign" establishes existence and "cause" shows why.

Return to item 7.

12. The statement is not false, because it is desirable to change from the present system to an alternative proposal if significant advantages or benefits can be achieved.

Return to item 3.

13. Correct. Next question: The first affirmative speaker should define all terms in a proposition.

If true, go to item 2.

If false, go to item 7.

14. The statement is not false, because the affirmative's answer to the third stock issue forecasts important benefits from a plan that is not yet in existence; thus, the benefits issue involves prediction.

Return to item 9.

15. Correct. Next question: The affirmative should avoid a complicated plan, but it should always provide ample details.

If true, go to item 9.

If false, go to item 5.

16. Correct. Next question: If a person is not close to a situation, his impartiality should lead to a good prediction.

If true, go to item 4.

If false, go to item 6.

17. The statement is not false, because the status quo usually has some serious problems. In fact, these problems are usually responsible for general interest in the proposition.

Return to item 1.

Arrange this partial outline of an affirmative case in logical order by placing the correct number in the appropriate blank.[2]

Resolved:_____
I.___ ___

  A._____

    1._____

    2._____

  B._____

    1._____

    2._____

II._____

  A._____

  B._____

III._____

  A._____

  B._____

  C._____

  D._____

1. States could pay better salaries to teachers, and
2. They give us talk instead of action, and
3. The affirmative proposes a national education plan:
4. That education in America demands immediate federal action.
5. The necessary funds would be provided by a party of action and not merely talk.
6. Many teachers are underpaid, many are on emergency certificates, and teachers are in short supply throughout the nation.
7. There is a need for a change in our present policies on education, for
8. A national program of college loans and scholarships would be created.
9. Significant benefits would result from the affirmative plan, for
10. They have permitted education to suffer from lack of financial support.
11. The Republicans have caused these problems, for
12. Federal funds for education would be allocated to the states, and
13. Students would be encouraged to become teachers by the college loans and scholarship programs, and
14. Many classrooms are overcrowded and many schoolhouses are unsafe, and
15. States could build the necessary facilities, and
16. The school situation is a national crisis, for

2. The case is based upon arguments presented by Adlai E. Stevenson in various speeches, written statements, and news conferences of the 1956 presidential campaign.

30 *Assignments*

For the sample debate in Appendix A:
1. Were the terms of the proposition defined adequately? Explain.
2. Outline the issues and contentions presented by the affirmative. Compare the organization with that suggested in this chapter.
3. Do you approve of presenting the plan in the first affirmative's constructive speech? Explain. Comment on the affirmative plan.
4. In what ways could the organization and development of the affirmative case be improved?

For the proposition you will be debating:
1. Give several reasonable definitions of the terms of the proposition.
2. Will the traditional case or the comparative-advantage case be more logical to use? Explain.
3. List the issues.
4. List some possible contentions that would support your position on the issues. Are the need arguments inherent indictments of the present system?

Suggested references

Capp, Glenn R., Robert Huber, and Wayne C. Eubank. "Duties of Affirmative Speakers—A Symposium," *The Speech Teacher*, VIII (March 1959), 139–149.

Newman, Robert P. "The Inherent and Compelling Need," *The Journal of the American Forensic Association*, II (May 1965), 66–71.

Seifrit, William. "The Affirmative Case: Principle or Plan?" *The AFA Register*, IX (Spring 1961), 5–10.

Wall, K. Wayne. "Three Concepts of the Affirmative Case," *The AFA Register*, IX (Spring 1961), 11–14.

CHAPTER THREE

Organizing the Negative Case

If the affirmative team presents a prima facie case, it overcomes, at least temporarily, the presumption of the negative. The objective of the negative team is to present a prima facie rejoinder—one that refutes the arguments of the affirmative and thus defeats the proposition—again, at least temporarily. This chapter discusses different types of negative cases; two involve a defense of the status quo, and two do not.

One of the most difficult problems a negative team faces is to achieve a proper balance between the refutation of the affirmative team's case and constructive arguments for its own position. The proper balance obviously depends a great deal on the case the affirmative develops. In preparing for a debate, therefore, the nega-

32   tive team must anticipate as best it can the kind of case the affirmative will present. Obviously, outlines for negative cases must be
tentative, because the negative must always be prepared to make
adaptations to the affirmative case.

Introducing the negative case

First of all, the negative either should accept the affirmative's
definitions of the key terms in the proposition or should explain
what definitions it will accept. As was suggested in Chapter 2, however, the negative should not quibble about the affirmative's definitions if they are reasonable.

Like the affirmative team, the negative should clarify its position at
the beginning of the debate. It should take a firm stand. If the negative team intends to defend the present system, the first negative
debater should say so in his opening remarks.

Furthermore, since so much of the negative's time is spent in
refutation and since refutation sometimes gives the impression of
lack of organization, the first negative speaker may wish to preview
the entire pattern of his team's case.

The traditional case

Because most affirmative teams organize their cases around the
stock issues of need, plan, and benefits, most negative teams use this
same pattern. This traditional negative case involves a total defense
of the present system *in principle*. As a member of the negative team
you may admit certain shortcomings in the present system, but you
should argue that the shortcomings are not inherent in the system,
that the principles of the present system are sound, and that the
present system is improving steadily.

Refuting the need. Because the negative, in the traditional case, is
committed to a defense of the present system, it contends that there
is no need to change to another system. To refute the affirmative's
need argument, the negative often argues that the affirmative has
made an incorrect or an incomplete analysis of the present system.
When compulsory health insurance for all citizens was the national
topic for intercollegiate debate, affirmative debaters had difficulty
showing a need for compulsory insurance for all groups. Consequently, negative debaters often were able to charge that the affirm-

ative debaters had made an incomplete analysis of the present system, because they had failed to analyze the needs of significant parts
of the population. The negative debaters usually further contended
that large segments of the population did not need compulsory
insurance and that the need was obviously not universal. By arguing
that the affirmative has made an incorrect or an incomplete analysis
of the present system, you, as a member of the negative team, not only
can conform to the organizational pattern established by the affirmative (assuming, of course, that the affirmative has organized its case
around the stock issues) but also can treat each affirmative contention from the negative point of view. As you refute each contention,
you can point to an incomplete or incorrect analysis and can conclude
that the affirmative arguments do not constitute a cause for changing
from the present system. Refutation, which is the destruction of
opposing proof, requires a sound knowledge of the tests of evidence
and reasoning. Chapter 5 will present these tests.

In the process of refuting the affirmative need arguments, the first
negative speaker may find it necessary to explain or to clarify certain
aspects of the present system. Should he give this explanation as part
of his refutation of the affirmative need arguments, or should he set
aside a specific segment of time later in his speech for this purpose?
A general rule, which admits to an occasional exception, would be to
provide the explanation or clarification while refuting the need
arguments. If the explanation is postponed until later in the speech,
its effectiveness in refuting the affirmative arguments may be ob-
scured. However, if the first negative has important, constructive
material not touched upon by the affirmative, he should present it
after his refutation of the affirmative's need arguments — unless this
material is required to clarify the negative's position at the outset.

If you choose both to refute the affirmative's need arguments and to
present a constructive defense of the present system, you might
organize the first part of your case in the following manner:

I. There is no need for a change, for
    A. The affirmative has made an incomplete or incorrect
       analysis of the present system, for
       1. Need #1 is not correct or logical, and
       2. Need #2 is not correct or logical.
    B. The principles of the present system are sound, for
       1. Description of structure of the present system.
         a. Evidence
         b. Evidence

2. Description of function of the present system.
            a. Evidence
            b. Evidence

In their need argument, the affirmative debaters usually cite numerous evils which they allege are inherent in the present system. You have at least two ways of attacking an *inherency argument*. One of these is treated in the discussion of the adjustments and repairs case (see pp. 37–38). In the other, you may agree to some shortcomings but will argue that they will disappear under the present system. Obviously, if the evils will not persist under the present system, they are not *inherent* in the system. In other words, the evils are not caused by the present system and so are not inherent arguments for changing the present system. At this point, you should cite other causes for the alleged evils, causes which would not be affected by the affirmative proposition.

You must be alert not to misinterpret the affirmative argument. Some affirmative teams argue that the conditions they wish to change are not *causes* of the evils, but rather are *contributing conditions* under which the evils can occur. For example, an affirmative team might assert that while United States' economic aid might not have caused the stagnation of a foreign country's economy, such aid encouraged dependency and thus made it difficult for the country to develop its own indigenous economic system. Here you should not attempt to disprove an inherency argument, because none was made. Instead, you should try to show that conditions other than the present system had a greater bearing on the alleged evils, and you should also point out that these conditions would not be corrected by the affirmative proposal.

Refuting the plan. The nature of a proposition will dictate whether a detailed plan will be a significant factor in an affirmative case. For a proposition recommending United States' recognition of Red China, the affirmative plan would probably have few details. For a proposition recommending a program of public works for the unemployed, the affirmative plan would probably be quite detailed. To refute a detailed affirmative plan, you should analyze it in terms of its structure, function, method of enforcement, etc. You might also prepare a list of items that should be included in any satisfactory plan and might scrutinize the affirmative plan in order to discover any omissions.

You could organize your refutation of the affirmative plan in the following manner:

II. The affirmative plan is not workable, for
    A.   Its structure has basic flaws, for
        1. Example
        2. Example
    B.   It cannot function effectively, for
        1. Example
        2. Example
    C.   It lacks effective enforcement, for
        1. Example
        2. Example

Refuting the benefits. You can approach the affirmative's benefits argument in three ways: (1) You can argue that the affirmative plan will not actually correct the evils the affirmative debaters have alleged are in the present system. (2) You can argue that the additional benefits the affirmative claims for its plan will not ensue. (3) You can argue that evils will be produced by the affirmative plan. The most basic question is: Will the affirmative plan solve or correct the problems or deficiencies the affirmative has cited in developing its need arguments? To raise this question is not an admission that there is a need for a change; it is simply a test of the logical adequacy of the affirmative case. Many negative teams, in their haste to cite the probable evils of the affirmative plan, neglect a thorough analysis of the affirmative's list of advantages. Analyze the affirmative's predictions with great care. Will the affirmative's plan solve the problems cited in its need argument? Will the additional benefits the affirmative lists actually follow from the plan? After you have refuted the benefits argument of the affirmative, then cite the evils you predict will result if the affirmative plan is adopted.

You might develop your refutation of the affirmative's benefits argument in the following manner:

III. The affirmative proposal will not be beneficial, for
    A. The plan will not correct the alleged problems cited in the present system, for
        1. Problem #1 is not corrected, for
          a. Evidence
        2. Problem #2 is not corrected, for
          a. Evidence
    B. The additional benefits the affirmative claims will not occur, for
        1. Benefit #1 will not occur, for

       a. Evidence
2. Benefit #2 will not occur, for
       a. Evidence
C. Undesirable effects will result from the affirmative proposal, for
    1. Evil #1 will occur, for
       a. Evidence
    2. Evil #2 will occur, for
       a. Evidence

Duties of speakers. In presenting the traditional case as just described, you and your partner may organize your two constructive speeches in the following way:

First negative	*Time*
1. Introduction to negative position and possible comment on definition of terms	2 minutes
2. Refutation of need	5 minutes
3. Arguments in defense of present system	2 minutes
4. Summary and conclusion	1 minute

Second negative	
1. Review of negative attack on need	2 minutes
2. Refutation of plan	2 minutes
3. Refutation of benefits and enumeration of the evils likely to occur	5 minutes
4. Summary and conclusion	1 minute

Sample negative case

The following skeleton case is based upon arguments presented by Dwight D. Eisenhower in the 1956 presidential campaign. His basic arguments have been adapted to the pattern of the traditional negative case. (Before studying this case, review the sample affirmative case on page 23.)

Resolved: That the United States should stop testing the hydrogen bomb.

I. There is no need for a change in our testing policy, for
 A. The affirmative has made an incorrect analysis of the present system, for
 1. The present rate of testing does not imperil the health of humanity, and
 2. In the past two years, the U.S. has made fourteen proposals for disarmament and control of nuclear weapons.
 B. The principles of the present system are sound, for
 1. Testing and developing nuclear weapons is a major deterrent to Soviet aggression, and
 2. The U.S. is constantly ready to disarm under supervised international agreements.
II. The affirmative plan is not workable, for
 A. A unilateral attempt to control the future use of atomic power is a theatrical national gesture, and
 B. There is no indication that Russia would stop its testing, and
 C. Even with large weapons, it is impossible to determine immediately the size and character of the explosion.
III. The affirmative proposal will not be beneficial, for
 A. The plan will not correct the alleged problems in the present system, for
 1. Strontium 90 is a product of smaller rather than larger weapons, and
 2. Unless there are supervised international agreements, trust and understanding will not be promoted among nuclear powers.
 B. The additional benefits the affirmative lists will not occur, for
 1. It is not a cold war victory to weaken the deterrent power of the U.S., and
 2. Military strength would be weakened, for
 a. We must test to find ways to use nuclear weapons for defense, and
 b. We must test to develop weapons with reduced fall-out.

The adjustments and repairs case

The traditional negative case and the adjustments and repairs case both defend the present system, and their patterns of refutation and constructive argument are almost identical. The difference is that in

38 the adjustments and repairs case, the negative agrees to certain shortcomings in the present system and *suggests specific adjustments and repairs which will correct these shortcomings* and still preserve the present system. If these shortcomings can be corrected within the framework of the present system, they are not inherent indictments of that system and are not causes for a change to the affirmative proposal. The adjustments proposed by the negative must be in terms of the present system and must be significantly short of the changes advocated in the affirmative's proposal; otherwise, the negative will be conceding too many arguments.

Some negative teams explain the adjustments and repairs case by an analogy to repairing a car. They argue that poor brakes or faulty spark plugs are not "needs" for buying a new car. Such faults can be adjusted and repaired so that the car will give excellent service. And these repairs and adjustments are significantly short of buying a new car.

Naturally, you must be sure that the shortcomings you recognize are not *inherent* in the present system. If they are, the affirmative has successfully indicted some of the basic principles of the present system. After admitting certain correctable deficiencies in the status quo, you should detail the proposed adjustments and repairs, should show how the present system would work with the corrections, and should enumerate the benefits of the present system as corrected.

The direct refutation case

The direct refutation case and the counter-plan case (see below) involve a non-defense of the status quo; that is, they *do not in any way attempt to defend the present system.* One could say that the direct refutation case supports the present system indirectly, because a defeat of the affirmative resolution would leave "things as they are." The direct refutation case is similar to the traditional negative case in terms of refutation, but its constructive argument is limited to predicting evils that would arise if the affirmative proposal were adopted. Except for the time given to discussion of evils resulting from the affirmative's proposal, the negative team's speeches are devoted exclusively to attacking the evidence and reasoning of the affirmative. Many debate judges dislike the direct refutation case, because the negative team defends nothing and devotes almost all of its speaking time to the criticism of opposing arguments.

Occasionally, a national debate proposition lends itself to the presentation of a counter-plan by the negative team. In the counter-plan case, you agree with the affirmative that there is need for a change, but you present your own solution to the problem. Most negative teams consider this kind of case too risky, because the negative, like the affirmative, must accept a burden of proof for its counter-proposition.

In developing the counter-plan case, you either can accept all or part of the affirmative's analysis of need, or can present your own analysis of need. If you choose the first alternative, you should accept only those contentions of need which your counter-plan corrects, and should subject the remaining contentions of need to direct refutation. Your counter-plan should be clearly different from that of the affirmative. If the two plans are close in principle, you virtually concede the debate. After you have presented your counter-plan and have enumerated the benefits of the plan, you should explain clearly how this plan is superior to the plan of the affirmative.

One negative team developed a counter-plan case in debating a proposition to place labor organizations under the jurisdiction of antitrust legislation. The negative team agreed with the affirmative's contention that labor unions had achieved a monopoly in the labor market and that they could cripple the nation's economy if they used this power unjustly. However, the negative team opposed subjecting the labor unions to antitrust regulations; instead, it proposed a counter-plan which combined a profit-sharing program with a guaranteed annual wage. This plan, the negative argued, would deprive labor of the motivation to strike; thus, labor's power would be curbed without the use of antitrust legislation. The negative, in this instance, developed an effective counter-plan case.

Sometimes the negative team which uses a counter-plan case presents a need of its own — if the affirmative gives what the negative believes is an unacceptable analysis of the present system or if the affirmative lists problems that could not be solved by the negative counter-plan. If the negative does present its own analysis of the need for a change, the debate can rapidly deteriorate into a situation in which the two teams are talking about two different subjects. Under these circumstances, most debate judges would vote for the affirmative team. Under the best of circumstances, the counter-plan case is risky; a negative team that decides to present one should be aware of its pitfalls.

40   *Attacking the comparative-advantage case*

If the present system has no serious faults, the affirmative may present a comparative-advantage case (see pp. 24–27). One pattern for the development of this case involves the discussion of qualities that are absent in the present system and the prediction of problems that the present system is not likely to solve. As a member of the negative team, you can use traditional patterns of refutation against this case, by analyzing critically the affirmative description of the present system and the affirmative's proposal and by appraising the probability of the affirmative predictions.

A second pattern for the affirmative comparative-advantage case discusses only additional benefits to be expected from the affirmative proposal. The affirmative team that uses this pattern is sometimes trying to circumvent the need issue. The best way to refute this form of the comparative-advantage case is to minimize the affirmative advantages or to show that the advantages can be achieved under the present system. This kind of refutation would probably force the affirmative into a detailed attack on the present system. If it does, you can then point out that the affirmative has virtually admitted a grave weakness in its original analysis of the status quo.

• The negative team as well as the affirmative team must be able to support the position it takes with evidence and reasoning. In the following chapter, "Supporting the Case: Evidence and Reasoning," methods of conducting research will be described and the basic kinds of evidence and reasoning will be explained.

Programed test

1. First question: The negative should delay making its position clear until it has heard both affirmative speakers.
    If true, go to item 15.
    If false, go to item 12.
2. Correct. Next question: When presenting a counter-plan case, the negative should accept only those need arguments that its plan corrects.
    If true, go to item 16.
    If false, go to item 14.
3. The statement is not true, because the adjustments and repairs case does involve a defense of the present system. It is the counter-plan and direct refutation cases that do not support the status quo.

Return to item 16.

4.   The statement is not false, because all negative cases are designed to prevent the adoption of the affirmative proposition; therefore, undesirable effects of the affirmative proposal can be used as part of any negative case.

Return to item 13.

5.   Correct. You have completed the programed test for Chapter 3.

6.   The statement is not true, because negative arguments should be used directly against affirmative arguments. The primary purpose of a negative case is to defeat the affirmative proposition, and so the true effect of negative arguments can be seen in refutation of the affirmative case.

Return to item 12.

7.   Correct. Next question: In an adjustments and repairs case, the negative can agree to any need argument so long as the problems cited in the affirmative's need argument are corrected by the repairs the negative proposes for the present system.

If true, go to item 10.

If false, go to item 17.

8.   The statement is not false, because judges normally prefer that a team at least suggest some positive action, and many of them expect the negative team to take advantage of its presumption.

Return to item 17.

9.   Correct. Next question: When the negative argues that the affirmative's plan will not correct the affirmative's need arguments, it is virtually admitting that the need does exist.

If true, go to item 11.

If false, go to item 13.

10. The statement is not true, because the affirmative's need arguments that are inherent indictments of the present system would necessitate changing some of the basic characteristics of the present system, and the adjustments and repairs case involves a defense of the basic principles of the status quo.

Return to item 7.

11. The statement is not true. The negative is evaluating the logical adequacy of the affirmative case — whether the plan corrects the alleged need. No admission of the correctness of the affirmative's need arguments is implied.

Return to item 9.

12. Correct. Next question: The true effect of a negative contention is revealed better in negative constructive argument than in refutation of the affirmative case.

42   *If true, go to item 6.*
       If false, go to item 9.

13. Correct. Next question: Any negative team can improve its case by arguing that undesirable effects would result from the affirmative proposition.
       If true, go to item 7.
       If false, go to item 4.

14. The statement is not false, because the negative's acceptance of an affirmative's need argument means that the negative expects to correct the problem in its counter-plan.
       Return to item 2.

15. The statement is not true, because the negative, like the affirmative, is expected to clarify its position at the outset of the debate. The negative should show the confidence it has in its case by revealing its position in the first negative's opening speech.
       Return to item 1.

16. Correct. Next question: The counter-plan case and the adjustments and repairs case involve a non-defense of the status quo.
       If true, go to item 3.
       If false, go to item 5.

17. Correct. Next question: Many judges dislike the direct refutation case.
       If true, go to item 2.
       If false, go to item 8.

Exercise

Arrange this partial outline of a traditional negative case in logical order by placing the correct number in the appropriate blank.[1]

Resolved:＿＿＿＿   1. The farmer will become a commodity open for political bids.

I.＿＿＿＿   2. It is based on a policy of expediency rather than on a policy of principle, and

　A.＿＿＿＿   3. That the farm program of the Democratic Party should be adopted.

　　1.＿＿＿＿   4. Food prices are increasing, and

　　　 5. Undesirable effects will result from the
　　2.＿＿＿＿   affirmative proposal, for

---

1. The case is based upon arguments presented by Dwight D. Eisenhower in various speeches, written statements, and news conferences of the 1956 presidential campaign.

B._____

1._____

2._____

II._____

A._____

B._____

III._____

A._____

B._____

6. The Democrats have made an incorrect analysis of the present system, for
7. Flexible price supports and conservation programs are matters of sound principle.
8. The Democratic program is not workable, for
9. The surplus will grow larger under high price supports, and
10. There is no need for a change in our present program, for
11. A policy of principle rather than a policy of expediency is followed, and
12. The surplus is diminishing.
13. High price supports did not solve the basic problems of agriculture under previous Democratic administrations.
14. The principles of the Republican program are sound, for

Assignments

For the sample debate in Appendix A:
1. What kind of negative case was presented? Explain.
2. Did the negative present a prima facie rejoinder in its first speech? Explain.
3. What is your reaction to the negative's delaying its analysis of the plan to the second negative speech?
4. In what ways could the organization and development of the negative case be improved?

For the proposition you will be debating:
1. Evaluate the possible use of each kind of negative case.
2. List some possible contentions that would support the present system.
3. List some possible disadvantages of the affirmative proposition.

Suggested references

Nebergall, Roger E. "The Negative Counterplan," *The Speech Teacher,* VI (September 1957), 217–220.

44   Patterson, J. W. "The Obligations of the Negative in a Policy Debate," *The Speech Teacher,* XI (September 1962), 208–213.

Thompson, Wayne N. "The Effect of a Counterplan Upon the Burden of Proof," *Central States Speech Journal,* XIII (Autumn 1962), 247–252.

CHAPTER FOUR

Supporting the Case: Evidence and Reasoning

Methods of research
Kinds of evidence
Kinds of reasoning
Bibliography of reference materials

The two previous chapters discuss ways of outlining affirmative and negative cases; this chapter describes methods of research and explains the basic kinds of evidence and reasoning used by both affirmative and negative debaters to support their arguments. To create a prima facie case or a prima facie rejoinder, you not only must be able to find good evidence but must know how to reason from it effectively.

Methods of research

You can never be a good debater unless you are willing to spend a great deal of time in re-search. A systematic procedure for investigating and recording important evidence and reasoning can be of inestimable help to

46   you as you attempt to analyze a proposition, discover the issues, and develop proofs. In the following suggested procedures, it is assumed that you as a member of a debating squad can share the tasks and the profits of research.

Begin with general reading. Do not underestimate the value of a broad, general knowledge of the debate topic. A wide background of information can help you evaluate accurately the material you uncover through more specific research and can enable you to place any given fact, opinion, or statistic in its proper perspective.

To help you decide upon good, general sources, consult an expert in the subject matter area of the debate topic. Often he can direct you to one or more references that will be of particular value to you. If the services of an expert are not readily available, consult the card catalog of your school library or examine various bibliographies. See pages 51–57 for a list of some good references.

Study the present system. Whether you intend to defend or attack the present system, make every effort to understand its structure and the way it functions. Study all existing laws and programs that relate to the system. Do not criticize the system hastily. First, be sure you understand it thoroughly. And as you study the history and background of the proposition, try to discover what characteristics of the present system may have aroused interest in the proposition.

Identify potential problem areas. As you read, you will discover that different authorities sometimes present contradictory points of view on the present system and on the proposition. Such conflicts of opinion suggest problem areas. At this stage of your research and analysis, try to identify all of these potential problem areas. Do not reject any problem as insignificant. Such rejections should be the joint decision of the debate squad, not that of a single debater. If a problem area is later rejected, the evidence that makes it ineffective should be recorded as resource material, so that it will be available if the opposing team should utilize the problem in its case.

Work individually and as a team on research. Make a comprehensive list of the issues and of the pro and con contentions. Divide these issues among the members of the debate squad. The scene is now set for each debater to do research in depth, to prepare skeleton debate cases, and to test his arguments in classroom discussion and debate.

After each member of the debate squad has done research on one or two of the issues, the group should begin sharing evidence. This pooling of evidence should provide each debater with material in depth on all potential problem areas in the proposition.

Prepare for a continuing pattern of research. As various arguments are presented by the affirmative and the negative in classroom discussions, list these arguments in an organized manner for all debaters to see and to use. As research continues throughout the year, add new problem areas or arguments to the list.

If a debate squad works well together, the members can share many of the continuing tasks in research. A single debater can seldom investigate all significant sources as they are published. But most, if not all, of these sources can be covered if they are divided among the members of the debate squad and each member reports to the squad any material he finds that is related to its list of potential arguments. Each debater, however, must understand thoroughly that he is responsible for the integrity and accuracy of any evidence he uses in the debate contest.

Record evidence carefully. Don't take notes hastily. First, read the entire chapter or article attentively so that you are sure you understand the author's meaning. Then write down any comments that you think will be useful to you. Do not write down quotations out of context. Include enough of the surrounding material so that the author's meaning is unmistakable.

Author
Author's qualifications
Article, magazine or book

"Problem Area"
Date and page

The Note

(If you quote the material directly, use quotation marks. If you paraphrase or summarize, place a "p" or an "s" in the corner of the card. Direct quotations are generally preferred in debate contests; when it is appropriate to paraphrase or summarize, be sure to do it fairly and objectively.)

48   Adopt a consistent pattern for recording and organizing your material. Some debaters use looseleaf notebooks with dividers for the various topics, but most prefer a file box with 4" x 6" or 5" x 7" index cards. If possible, type all notes; if not, be sure that you write clearly enough so that you as well as the other members of your squad can read your materials. Be sure that you take down quotations accurately and that you record full information about your source — author; author's qualifications; article, magazine or book; publication date and page. Study the sample index card for suggested placement of the required information and for further directions about recording material.

Kinds of evidence

Evidence, the basic raw material of argumentation and debate, is usually made up of *facts, expert opinions,* and *statistics.* Actual objects are seldom used in academic debates. However, on occasion, maps, charts, graphs, etc., can be very effective in clarifying material and should never be ruled out as possible adjuncts to explanations and descriptions.

Facts. The term *fact* is somewhat difficult to define, but it normally refers to objective statements and empirically verifiable data. For example: "Three-fourths of the students in our university are pro-Republican." "Many of the rivers and lakes in the United States are no longer safe for swimming because of industrial pollution." Such "facts" can be subjected to various kinds of tests to check their correctness. (See Chapter 5, pp. 61 – 64, for an explanation of methods for testing facts.) Any energetic investigator can discover facts to support his case, and any one can verify those facts through appropriate methods. Normally, the facts used in educational debate are found in periodical, governmental, and scholarly sources.

Expert opinion. The second kind of evidence, the *expert opinion,* is a judgment by a person whose knowledge and experience qualify him as an authority. For example, an audience would probably be inclined to take quite seriously this kind of statement from a man who had been president of the institution for a number of years: "Our university will have an enrollment of 20,000 by fall 1975." Or this statement by a well-trained, experienced chemical engineer: "Within one year, Blank Lake would be safe for swimmers if all the industries located on its shores would treat their wastes by the Morgan

Method." Sometimes the opinion of a competent and reliable lay person may be used, but normally such a person is cited only as a source for factual information. Expert opinion is usually presented to clarify special problems, relationships, or technical data. Because the worth of an opinion as proof is directly related to the quality and reliability of its source, debaters should take care to select the most reputable authorities available. (See page 62 for tests of opinion.)

Statistics. When facts and opinions are analyzed, organized, and quantified, the results are called *statistics.* While a single fact or opinion may be sufficient proof for a specific case, a compilation of facts or opinions often has greater value. An example of one person who cannot afford voluntary health insurance is meaningful, but statistical data on the entire population are far more significant to most audiences. Statistics based on factual data are the most useful to a debater; they can be found in various governmental publications, as well as in other publications. One of the most important governmental publications is the *Statistical Abstract of the United States.* The opinion poll is the most common source of quantified opinion. (See page 63 for tests of statistics.)

Kinds of reasoning

While evidence is made up of facts, opinions, and statistics, reasoning is based on interpretation of facts, opinions, and statistics. In other words, evidence is the raw material from which reasoning is constructed. In the following pages four different modes of reasoning will be described. These modes of reasoning are not mutually exclusive; any one mode may contain one or more of the other modes to varying degrees. The following descriptions, though, will be based upon the principal characteristics of the mode under consideration.

Sign. In reasoning from sign (see page 18), you infer from the presence or absence of one fact the presence or absence of another fact. These relations, which are sometimes referred to as correlative relations, establish the *existence* of something and not the reason why it exists. Sign reasoning can also be described as a substance-attribute relationship, which means that the presence of a substance assures the presence of certain attributes of that substance, or vice versa. The presence of a picket line in front of a factory usually means that a strike is in progress; the picket line did not cause the strike,

50   but it is a sign of its existence. The Cuban Crisis of 1962 was a sign of the "cold war," but it did not cause the "war." A doctor observes certain signs, or symptoms, to determine what disease is present in a person. In all of these examples, the existence of one fact is asserted by noting the existence of another fact.

Cause. In reasoning from cause (see page 18), you relate two or more items to each other in such a way as to demonstrate that one or more of the items is the cause of the existence of the other item or items. You may take a given result or effect and attempt to determine what caused it, or you may take a certain "cause" and attempt to project an effect that will result from it. In short, you may reason from cause to effect or from effect to cause. Affirmative teams usually cite evils in the present system and attempt to prove that they are caused by inherent characteristics of the system. They also usually contend that their proposal will produce or cause certain benefits. For example, advocates of the trimester and quarter systems often argue that their systems will produce or cause more efficient use of school facilities than can be attained in a semester system. Negative teams make use of causal reasoning by predicting undesirable effects of the affirmative proposal. They might argue that the trimester and quarter systems would create an undesirable situation, for students under such a system would not have enough time to think over and absorb the subject matter they have studied. Furthermore, they might challenge the validity of the affirmative's causal reasoning. They might agree with the affirmative's account of the evils in the semester plan but might, through their own causal reasoning, attempt to show that the evils were temporary and not caused by inherent characteristics of the system.

Example. Reasoning from example is often called reasoning by generalization. In reasoning from example, you examine one or more items from a certain class and then draw a general conclusion about the entire class, or at least about a larger number of members than were included in the sample. For instance, you might investigate several typical low-income families and discover that none of the children of these families had been able to go to college. As a result of this discovery, you might conclude that no, or at least few, children of low-income families are able to go to college. After you have established a sign or causal relationship, you may use examples to show that the relationship occurs often enough to justify action.

Analogy. In analogical reasoning, you infer that when two items, 51
cases, or happenings are alike in some respects, they will be alike in
other respects. If something is known to be true about the one, the
same thing is inferred to be true about the other. If the items, cases,
or happenings are from the same general class, the resultant analogy
is described as *literal* and it has probative force. If they are from
different classes, the analogy is described as *figurative* and should be
used for illustrative purposes only. You would be using a literal
analogy if you argued that the United States would have good results
if it nationalized its basic industries, because Great Britain had
nationalized its basic industries with "good" results. Here you
would be comparing two countries and inferring that what was good
for one would be good for the other. You would be using a figurative
analogy if you argued that nations need new ideas even as the earth
needs rain, since you would be comparing items from two different
classes — nations and the earth.

• If you study the available references on your topic you should be
able to find abundant evidence (facts, opinions, and statistics) and to
develop valid reasoning in order to create a prima facie case or a
prima facie rejoinder. To check the strength of your own case and to
challenge the case of your opponents, you must be able to use the tests
for evidence and reasoning. Such ability will help you destroy opposing proofs and defend your own — will help you engage successfully in refutation and rebuttal, which is the concern of the following
chapter.

Bibliography of reference materials

A. *General Sources*
 1. Card catalog of your school or city library
    A complete listing of books (General Catalog) and periodical
    and society publications (Serial Catalog) that are available in
    your library.
 2. *Encyclopaedia Britannica*
    A survey of all fields of knowledge. Be sure to check the
    annual supplements which keep it up to date.
 3. *Encyclopedia Americana*
    A survey of all fields of knowledge with special emphasis on
    information about the United States. It also publishes an
    annual supplement.
 4. *Guide to Reference Books* by Constance M. Winchell

A guide for locating and evaluating specific reference works.
  5. *United States Library of Congress Catalog of Printed Cards*
     A guide to all books in the Library of Congress. It is organized under various subject headings.

B. *Important Indexes*
  1. *Agricultural Index*
     A guide to selected periodicals and bulletins on agricultural and related subjects. (See item 5 below.)
  2. *Applied Science and Technology Index*
     A guide to periodicals in various scientific and technological fields, including automation, engineering, industrial and mechanical arts, transportation, and others.
  3. *Bibliographic Index*
     A bibliography of bibliographies. It can lead you to important sources on a variety of subjects.
  4. *Biography Index*
     An index of biographical information in books and magazines.
  5. *Biological and Agricultural Index*
     Same publication as *Agricultural Index*. Title was changed in 1964. It now has a better balance between biological and agricultural subjects.
  6. *Business Periodicals Index*
     A subject index to all fields of business, finance, economics, management, etc.
  7. *Cumulative Book Index*
     A record of all books published in English.
  8. *Education Index*
     A guide to books and periodicals on education.
  9. *Index to Legal Periodicals*
     A subject and author index to articles on law and courtroom decisions.
  10. *International Index*
     A guide to scholarly journals in the humanities and social sciences.
  11. *London Times: Official Index*
     A source for articles appearing in the *Times*. Indexing is by date, page, and column.
  12. *Monthly Checklist of State Publications*
     A listing of many publications under the name of the issuing state, territory, or possession.

13. *New York Times Index*
    A good source for newspaper articles on any topic. Indexing is by date, page, and column; cross-referencing is also provided.
14. *Public Affairs Information Service*
    An index of books, magazines, documents, and pamphlets for materials on social issues, economics, political science, and others.
15. *Reader's Guide to Periodical Literature*
    A subject, author, and title index to general and popular magazines, although some scientific and scholarly periodicals are also indexed.
16. *United Nations Documents Index*
    An index to publications issued by the United Nations.
17. *United States Government Publications: Monthly Catalog*
    A listing of publications by the Federal Government. Includes federal documents, both congressional and departmental.
18. *Vertical File Index*
    A general index for pamphlets and leaflets. Includes prices and directions for ordering.

C. *Yearbooks, Almanacs, etc.*
    1. *Annual Register of World Events*
       Reviews the events of a year with emphasis on the affairs of England.
    2. *Book of the States*
       Contains statistical information and excellent articles on various phases of state government.
    3. *Facts on File*
       A summary of the events of a week under various headings. Contains indexing and cross-referencing.
    4. *Information Please Almanac*
       A wide variety of statistical and factual information on the United States and the world.
    5. *Keesing's Contemporary Archives*
       The English version of *Facts on File*.
    6. *Statesman's Year-Book*
       A source of statistical information on all countries of the world.
    7. *Statistical Abstract of the United States*
       A source of statistical data on the United States.
    8. *World Almanac and Book of Facts*

54   A source of factual information on a wide variety of subjects. Contains excellent indexing.

D. *Serial Publications on Current Topics*
1. *The Annals of the American Academy of Political and Social Science*
Contains authoritative articles on specific problems in national and international affairs.
2. *Asian Recorder*
A summary of the events of each week in twenty-six Asian countries. Includes an index.
3. *Congressional Digest*
A monthly presentation of one controversial subject, including pro and con arguments. One issue is devoted each year to the high school debate topic and another to the college debate proposition.
4. *Current History*
A source for articles on the national and international scene.
5. *Federal Reserve Bulletin*
Presents extensive information and data on economic and financial conditions in the United States.
6. *Headline Series* (Foreign Policy Association)
A series of pamphlets on specific problems and issues in world affairs.
7. *Labor Law Reporter*
Contains articles on labor relations and the law.
8. *Public Affairs Pamphlets*
A bulletin of the United States Office of Education which indexes many available pamphlets.
9. *Reference Shelf*
A series of books, each of which has a thorough accounting of articles, books, pro and con positions, and bibliography for a single, controversial question.

E. *Specialized Reference Aids*
1. *Congressional Record*
A daily record of Congressional debates along with other materials a Congressman may wish to insert. It does not contain the texts of bills.
2. Current periodicals, newspapers, and books not yet indexed. Your best way of locating the most recent materials.
3. *Dissertation Abstracts*

A listing in abstract form of the doctoral dissertations of 117 universities.
4. *Encyclopedia of the Social Sciences*
Includes virtually any subject related to the social sciences. All materials are prepared by experts and are particularly valuable for background information.
5. *International Who's Who*
Includes biographies of men and women of all nations.
6. Library of Congress publication on the annual college debate proposition.
Write to your Senator or Representative for free copies.
7. *Special Analysis of the American Enterprise Institute for Public Policy Research*
A useful and authoritative publication on the national intercollegiate debate proposition.
8. *The NUEA Discussion and Debate Manual*
Contains articles and reprints on the high school debate topic.
9. *Who's Who*
Lists outstanding living British citizens, plus a few prominent people of other nationalities.
10. *Who's Who in America*
The American version of *Who's Who*.

Programed test

1. First question: Debaters should not engage in general reading; they should begin their research by reading specific references to specific issues.
If true, go to item 11.
If false, go to item 14.
2. The statement is not true, because the interpretation of facts, opinions, and statistics is called reasoning.
Return to item 16.
3. Correct. Next question: Causal reasoning is used to test the inherency of the affirmative's need arguments.
If true, go to item 12.
If false, go to item 10.
4. The statement is not true, because a literal analogy does have probative force; it is the figurative analogy that lacks probative force.
Return to item 12.
5. Correct. Next question: Evidence is the raw material from which

56   reasoning is constructed.
       If true, go to item 17.
       If false, go to item 15.
6.   The statement is not false, because a correlation is a relationship between two things or happenings. Sign relations involve a relationship between the presence or absence of certain facts and the presence or absence of other facts; or a relationship between the presence or absence of substances and their attributes.
       Return to item 17.
7.   Correct. Next question: The quality and reliability of an authority are directly related to his worth as proof.
       If true, go to item 16.
       If false, go to item 13.
8.   Correct. You have completed the programed test for Chapter 4.
9.   The statement is not true, because a direct quotation is more accurate and reliable than a paraphrase or summary. Use the paraphrase or summary to construct the background of an expert's remarks, but use his actual words for the crucial area of proof.
       Return to item 14.
10. The statement is not false, because an affirmative team must trace significant shortcomings to basic characteristics of the present system. If the status quo does not cause these shortcomings, then an inherent indictment has not been presented by the affirmative.
       Return to item 3.
11. The statement is not true, because general knowledge of the proposition can help debaters analyze and evaluate specific items of information.
       Return to item 1.
12. Correct. Next question: A literal analogy has no probative force.
       If true, go to item 4.
       If false, go to item 8.
13. The statement is not false, because the more knowledge and experience an authority has, the more probative force his remarks will have. Debaters should not select a person simply because he agrees with them; they should select a reputable authority.
       Return to item 7.
14. Correct. Next question: Direct quotations of experts are usually too long; debaters should paraphrase or summarize such remarks.
       If true, go to item 9.
       If false, go to item 7.
15. The statement is not false, because facts, opinions, and statistics are the raw materials which a person interprets in order to arrive at

probable conclusions. These interpretations are called reasoning.
  Return to item 5.
16. Correct. Next question: Evidence consists of interpretations of facts, opinions, and statistics.
  If true, go to item 2.
  If false, go to item 5.
17. Correct. Next question: Sign relations are sometimes referred to as correlative relations.
  If true, go to item 3.
  If false, go to item 6.

Exercise

Identify the following samples of reasoning as sign, cause, example, or analogy.[1]

Kind   Sample

_____1. In answering Democratic charges of corruption in his administration, Eisenhower warned that a man should never mention rope in the house of one who had been hanged.

_____2. The smoky fury of our factories, the thousands of miles of new roads, and people working everywhere are evidence of a vigorous and dynamic people in America.

_____3. The Republican program of flexible price supports has brought about a decline in farm income.

_____4. The Democrats have used the hit-and-run statement; first, they accused the administration of lending money to Perón, but when they found out that the previous Democratic administration had lent the money, they ran in silence on the high, high road.

_____5. The Republicans must be in office, for the stock market is at the top and farm prices are at the bottom.

_____6. The minimum wage must not be increased until it can be extended to more people; if the minimum wage is extended after it is very high, then many concerns will be driven out of business.

_____7. If the termination of H-bomb tests by the U.S. would affect our military strength, then the stopping of tests by the

1. These are actual arguments presented by Dwight D. Eisenhower and Adlai E. Stevenson in various speeches, written statements, and news conferences in the 1956 presidential campaign.

58 Soviet Union would have a similar effect on their military strength. _____8. The Republicans have been using "under-cover" methods to undermine the progress of the country, for a declared enemy of public housing was placed in charge of public housing, an opponent of the federal income tax was placed in charge of the Bureau of Internal Revenue, and a man who fought against conservation was made Assistant Secretary of the Interior.

Assignments

For the sample debate in Appendix A:
1. Cite several examples of the kinds of evidence used in the debate.
2. Cite several examples of the kinds of reasoning used in the debate.
3. Prepare a sample evidence card for each kind of evidence used in the debate.

For the proposition you will be debating:
1. Select a general source and begin your research. Prepare three evidence cards.
2. Describe the present system.
3. Select the affirmative or negative side on one issue; do research in depth; organize your material; and present it orally in class.

Suggested references

Dresser, William R. "Studies of the Effects of Evidence: Implications for Forensics," *The AFA Register*, X (Fall 1962), 14–19.

Fotheringham, Wallace. "The Law of Evidence and the Debater," *The AFA Register*, VI (Spring 1958), 18–36.

Giffin, Kim, and Paul R. McKee. "An Analysis of Evidence in Debates," *The AFA Register*, X (Winter 1962), 1–5.

Judd, Larry, and Jerry Crenshaw. "Toward a Systematic Approach to Evidence," *Today's Speech*, XII (November 1964), 15–16.

Smith, William S. "Formal Logic in Debate," *The Southern Speech Journal*, XXVII (Summer 1962), 330–338.

Tarver, Jerry L. "Reflections on a New Debate Handbook," *The Journal of the American Forensic Association*, II (January 1965), 25–27.

Yeager, Raymond. "Aristotle's Topics as Sources of Proof," *The AFA Register*, V (Convention Reports Issue 1957), 4–7.

CHAPTER FIVE

Attack and Defense: Refutation and Rebuttal

Determining the major arguments
Tracing the arguments
Testing the evidence
Testing the reasoning
Patterns for refutation and rebuttal
A word about strategy

Refutation, which is commonly defined as the destruction of opposing proofs, is used in both attack and defense. *Attack* is "primary" refutation, since it involves the initial indictments of the opposition's case (see Chapter 3). *Defense* is "secondary" refutation, since it involves the refutation of refutation.

Rebuttal, which is a specific application of refutation, is conducted during special periods set aside for analysis of arguments presented in the constructive speeches (see Chapter 1 for an outline of the order and time limits of rebuttal speeches).

To engage successfully in refutation and rebuttal, you must be able to identify the main arguments of the debate, to trace them step by step as they are taken up

60 in the successive speeches, and to apply the appropriate tests for evidence and reasoning. Further, you should be able to organize your refutation and your rebuttal speeches in a clear and effective fashion. And, finally, you should be familiar with strategy devices so that you can expose and demolish them if they are used against you.

Determining the major arguments

Since you could not possibly cover all the arguments in the speaking time allotted to you, you must decide which arguments are most important and then concentrate on them in your refutation and rebuttal. Some debaters make the mistake of trying to refute every single argument presented by their opponents, and, consequently, are often unable to give sufficient time to the really crucial questions.

The affirmative's refutation. If the affirmative debaters analyze and investigate the proposition carefully, they should be able to discover the issues and to determine the major arguments and the evidence and reasoning for a prima facie case — the strongest possible foundation from which to launch their refutation. In refuting the arguments of the negative, the affirmative should always, if possible, relate them to the affirmative case. For example, when the debate topic was compulsory health insurance, negative debaters often contended that a program of compulsory health insurance would ruin private insurance companies. However, many affirmative debaters used private insurance companies in their plan for compulsory health insurance. And so, by citing the provisions of their plan, the affirmative could refute this indictment of the negative. Obviously, the negative may present indictments that are not provided for in the affirmative case. If the affirmative cannot answer the negative charges in terms of the affirmative case, it must then use direct refutation — by challenging the evidence or reasoning of the negative (see pages 61–67).

The negative's refutation. A complete defense of the status quo is usually the strongest foundation from which the negative may attack the affirmative case. In refuting the arguments of the affirmative, the negative can often relate them to the structure and functions of the present system. When the debate proposition was "Resolved: That the federal government should guarantee an opportunity for higher education to all qualified high-school graduates," some affirmative debaters indicted the present system on the grounds that the National Defense Education Act did not guarantee higher education to all qualified high-school graduates. Many negative debaters would refute this argument by describing other sources of financial aid and by demonstrating that the NDEA was just *one part* of the present system. Examining the affirmative contention in terms of the total present sources of financial aid enabled the negative to minimize what would seem at first to be a very effective argument. A word of caution: Regardless of a negative debater's eagerness to put affirmative arguments into a negative perspective, he should usually answer affirmative arguments in the order in which the affirmative presents them. The real impact of the negative's refutation will then be more obvious.

Tracing the arguments

In the course of a debate, some arguments or contentions may become so significant that they are discussed by every speaker in every speech. In a poor debate, the affirmative will state its case and then merely repeat it in subsequent speeches. Likewise, the negative will present its refutation and continue repeating it as the debate proceeds. In a good debate, however, the main arguments will be carried forward by each speaker as each side in turn accepts its burden of rebuttal. An affirmative team that can trace the development of an argument and show how it withstood negative refutation is revealing the true strength of its case. Similarly, a negative team that can trace an affirmative argument from its initial presentation to its final refutation is seriously weakening the affirmative case. (See the next chapter for methods of notetaking that will aid a debater in tracing the development of an argument throughout a debate.)

Debaters need to be able to review and summarize. Good debating is cumulative, because each speaker in each successive speech includes additional materials, either constructive arguments or refutation of arguments already presented.

Testing the evidence

You should be able to test the evidence and reasoning in your own case as well as that in the case of your opponents. If you have subjected your own case to careful testing, you will be equipped not only to deal with the refutation of the opposing team but also to launch an effective attack against their case. Another word of caution: Do not

62   treat evidence and reasoning as isolated points of refutation; instead,
treat them in terms of the issues, the vital questions upon which the
debate hinges.

The tests of evidence (facts, opinions, statistics) discussed in the
following pages are general questions that can be raised about most
kinds of evidence — your own as well as that of your opponents.
Remember that you will be able to answer some of these questions
from your own experience and common sense — and will be able to
convince the audience of the correctness of your answers by appeal-
ing in turn to their own experience and common sense. Many of the
questions, though, can be answered satisfactorily only by citing good
sources (see list of references on pp. 51–55). For example, if you question the reliability of the source of an opinion your opponent has
cited, you can insist that he produce satisfactory credentials for his
source.

Assume that you are participating in an interscholastic debate.
When your opponent presents some evidence to support his contention, here are questions you can raise:

1. *The facts.* Is the fact true, so far as you can judge?
   a) Is the fact consistent with known, established facts?
   b) Is the fact consistent with other facts presented by the same
   debate team?
   c) Is the fact consistent with human nature and experience?
2. *The source.* Is the source reliable and authoritative?
   a) *Of a fact.* Is the source capable of describing the fact accurately?
   For example, you wouldn't trust a color-blind person's testimony
   regarding colors, or a mentally retarded person's testimony regarding a complex sequence of events, or a known perjurer's
   testimony regarding almost anything.
   b) *Of an expert opinion.* Does the source have sufficient knowledge
   and experience to qualify him as an expert in the subject under
   consideration? Has his position on the subject been consistent? If
   not, does the quoted opinion represent his present position? Is he
   recognized as an expert by the audience? (This last question is
   particularly important when you are testing evidence for your own
   case, but it can also be useful if your opponents cite an opinion of
   a person whose views are commonly regarded as radical or unor-
   thodox.)
   c) *A magazine or newspaper.* If the source is the editorial or repor-
   torial staff of a magazine or newspaper, its reliability must be

judged by the past performance of the magazine or newspaper.
Since it is sometimes difficult to apply tests accurately to staff-prepared articles, such sources should be quoted with caution. You can, though, always ask: Does the magazine or newspaper have a reputation for careful reporting of fact and opinion and, in general, for honesty and impartiality? If an editorial is cited, you can always ask if the newspaper or magazine has a strong bias which is generally reflected in its editorial pages.

d) *Surveys.* Surveys, which are a particular kind of statistical evidence, should be subjected to careful analysis. For purposes of evaluation, the following questions can be raised:

1) Have a sufficient number of people been questioned? Has the survey been conducted in a small community, or in a certain section of the country? Have the results been projected to the nation?

2) Have the people questioned been representative of the population? If the sample in the survey is not a typical segment of the people being studied, then its extension to any other segments of the population is not justified.

3) Have any other factors influenced the results? Are the investigators biased? Has the survey been conducted at a time of day or year which would preclude reliable results? Were there any special conditions or did any incidents occur which affected and changed the results?[1]

3. *Recency.* Is the evidence up-to-date?

4. *Counter-evidence.* Is counter-evidence available? Do different sources report different statistics? Do different authorities reach different conclusions?

5. *So what?* In using the "so what?" test, you ask: Does the evidence prove what the opposition says it does? Assuming the evidence to be true, does it really prove the opposition's contention? While analyzing the proposition, most debaters create strong arguments that must be supported by evidence. Frequently, they do not find evidence that fits their arguments perfectly. Try to avoid this weakness in your own case. And be alert for this weakness in your opponents' case and exploit it whenever possible. For example, when the debate topic concerned federal aid to college students, one negative team argued that there was no need to increase

1. In Chapter 2, the elements of a good prediction were explained. Because predictions involve both evidence and reasoning, the tests of a good prediction should be reviewed in connection with this chapter: How close is the person to the situation? What degree of control does he have over the situation? To what extent are variable factors recognized and accounted for? Is there historical precedent?

64   financial aid to college students. As evidence for their contention, they cited figures which showed that family income was rising faster than college tuition. An alert affirmative team quickly pointed out that the negative's evidence didn't necessarily prove their contention. The affirmative insisted, rightly, that the negative should have compared the present *disposable* family income with present *total* college costs.

Evaluation of the methods of challenging evidence. Discovering and presenting counter-evidence is the easiest task in debating. Unfortunately, most debaters rely almost exclusively upon this kind of refutation. Observe a debate and notice how the debaters "leap" for their file boxes every time the opposing team reads some evidence.

Questioning the source of the evidence is also relatively easy. Questioning the recency of the evidence is also easy — and may result in a telling indictment against the opposition's case, if the evidence turns out to be dated.

Applying the "so what?" test is probably most difficult and also probably most rewarding. The outstanding debater always analyzes what the evidence says and tests its applicability to the argument being presented. The mere introduction of counter-evidence can only produce a stalemate, unless the challenging team at the same time can successfully bring into question the reliability of the source of the opposing team's evidence, or unless the counter-evidence becomes preponderate. It is better first to destroy the opposition's evidence in terms of different statistical assumptions, different dates, and different value assumptions and then to erect your own counter-evidence. You are now in a much stronger position than a stalemate, and the opposition will have to spend a great deal of time in rebuilding its case.

Testing the reasoning

Testing reasoning is more difficult than testing evidence, because the kinds of reasoning are not so easy to discern as the kinds of evidence. And identifying the kind of reasoning being used by one's opponent is only the beginning of careful analysis. The debater must also be able to discover any weakness in the opponent's reasoning and must know how to demonstrate this weakness to the audience.

Assumptions. In testing reasoning, debaters should first try to discover the opposition's assumptions. Many affirmative teams build their cases around a basic assumption. For example, in the debate topic on federal aid to college students, the affirmative usually assumes that *everyone should have a college education if he desires it.* As must be obvious, that assumption is not shared by all people. A negative team might decide to challenge it. Certainly arguments are available on each side of this question.

Some teams at the outset of the debate reveal their assumptions and ask the opposition's concurrence. On the other hand, some teams either conceal or are unaware of the assumptions that are vital to their case. Therefore, the first question to raise about an opponent's case is: Has the opposition made any basic assumptions which need proof? In addition to this general test, you should use the following tests for specific forms of reasoning (see Chapter 4 for an explanation of these forms).

Sign reasoning. To evaluate the relationship involved in an argument from sign, you can raise these questions:

1. *Has the generalization which underlies the sign reasoning been proved?* If a person argues that a union is on strike because he sees a picket line in front of a factory, then he is assuming this generalization: A picket line is formed only when there is a strike. Is this generalization true?
2. *Have a sufficient number of signs been presented?* Sometimes the correlation between a sign and a conclusion is very high, so that one sign is adequate evidence. Usually the conclusion is more certain and reliable if several signs are presented. The greater number of symptoms, for example, the more reliable the doctor's diagnosis is.

   Although other tests of sign reasoning are available, evaluating the generalization which underlies the sign will ordinarily yield the crucial materials for effective refutation. Testing the assumed generalization should reveal whether or not the sign relationship is only accidental or whether or not special circumstances have altered normal conditions. Certainly a conclusion is more reliable if a debater can point to many signs to justify his conclusion.

Causal reasoning. While a valid sign can establish the *existence* of a certain condition or problem, causal relations must be established to show *why* the condition or problem exists. The validity of these relationships can be tested by the following questions:

66   1. *Is there actually a causal relationship between the cited cause and alleged effect?* The fact that one event followed another does not mean that it was caused by the other. A form of severe, abnormal weather follows a series of nuclear tests. Did one event cause the other? A *direct* relationship between two events must be established if one is to be labeled as the cause of the other.

2. *Are there other more significant causes?* Remember that no event occurs in a vacuum. Most events have multiple causes; that is, most effects result from the functioning of many causes. A crucial question for the debater is: Are any of these other causes more significant than the ones presented by the opposition?

3. *Are there any other effects?* Are these "other effects" desirable or undesirable? For example, the negative may ask: Will the affirmative plan create new and greater evils? And the affirmative may ask: Are the advantages of the present system obviated by significant disadvantages?

4. *Will intervening causes prevent the predicted effect from occurring?* Farm surpluses can be predicted on the basis of current production, consumption, and distribution rates. But other factors might intervene to alter the results. A severe drought or the sale of large quantities of foodstuffs to foreign nations could diminish significantly, or even eliminate, the surplus.

Reasoning from example. Ordinarily, a debater refutes reasoning from an example to a descriptive generalization by showing that the opposition has made an incomplete analysis. You will notice that the following questions which test this kind of reasoning are very similar to the questions used to test survey evidence, since reasoning from example is used in the formulation of survey evidence.

1. *Have a sufficient number of examples been presented?* Debaters who draw a conclusion from a limited sample may commit the fallacy of "hasty generalization." Of course, it is difficult to say what a "sufficient number" of examples is because number is closely related to the typicality of the sample. In general, relatively few examples will be needed for a generalization about a homogeneous population; many examples will be needed for a generalization about a heterogeneous population.

2. *Are the examples representative?* This is the most important test for this kind of reasoning. If the examples are representative or typical of the total population, then the conclusion about the population becomes quite reliable.

3. *Are negative instances accounted for?* Has the debater engaged in biased reporting? Has he ignored those examples which might disprove his generalization? A reliable analysis would include a sufficient number of representative examples and would also recognize and account for the notable exceptions. As a matter of fact, accounting for negative instances strengthens rather than weakens a debater's case.

Analogical reasoning. As explained in Chapter 4, there are two kinds of analogies: the literal analogy which involves a comparison of objects, events, or happenings *from the same class;* and the figurative analogy which involves a comparison of objects, events, or happenings *from different classes.* Because the figurative analogy is used for illustrative purposes rather than for proof, the following questions apply only to literal analogies:

1. *Are the compared items alike in essential respects?* The important term in this test is *essential.* Obviously, there will always be some differences between compared items; true identity cannot exist between items, cases, or happenings. Certain likenesses, however, will be vital to the inference being made. These likenesses must exist to make the conclusion warrantable. For example, if a person infers that a certain lake area will make a popular summer resort simply because another lake area has become a popular resort, he must be sure that all the conditions contributing to the popularity of the one area are also present in the other area.
2. *Are major differences accounted for?* Sometimes compared items may differ in major ways, but these differences do not significantly affect the strength of the analogical reasoning. However, unless these differences are accounted for in some way, the asserted relationship may be weakened. Acknowledging major differences and placing them in proper perspective can prevent your opponent from making obvious attacks on your reasoning. Because it is relatively easy to discover significant differences and often quite time-consuming to account satisfactorily for them, most debaters usually avoid the analogy as a form of support for their major contentions.

Patterns for refutation and rebuttal

Because of the complexity of a debate contest, it is impossible to prescribe exact organizational patterns for the many refutation and rebuttal situations that will arise. The following suggestions, how-ever, can provide a basic framework, though they will have to be adapted to the content of a specific debate.

Refutation. You will have occasion to use refutation frequently and throughout the entire debate. In general, follow this procedure in refuting your opponent's proof:

1. Identify the proof to be refuted.
2. "Destroy" the proof by attacking the opponent's supporting evidence or reasoning.
3. Explain the impact of your refutation on the debate as a whole.

If an item of proof is particularly significant in a debate, you should make its importance clear in step one, when you identify the proof. The third step then shows "what it means" to the debate.

Rebuttal speeches. As Chapter 1 explained, the last part of a debate (usually twenty minutes) is given over to rebuttal speeches, and each debater ordinarily has five minutes in which to defend or rebuild his own case and to launch a final attack against the case of his oppo-nents. It is fairly common practice for both affirmative and negative debaters to organize their rebuttal speeches around the stock issues in the following pattern:

1. Review the arguments raised regarding the need issue, and carry them forward with attack or defense.
2. Review the arguments raised regarding the plan, and carry them forward with attack or defense.
3. Review the arguments raised regarding the benefits issue, and carry them forward with attack or defense.

Note that the affirmative must re-establish its case and must also answer the major objections of the negative. Similarly, the negative must briefly restate its major objections to the principal contentions of the affirmative.

A word about strategy

Strategy in debate often suggests the use of tricks or schemes to get the better of one's opponents. Negative teams sometimes make many trivial attacks on an affirmative case or raise many questions of doubtful importance. Their intent is to present so many arguments or so many questions that the affirmative will not have time to answer them all. The negative can then claim that the affirmative has failed to solve some crucial problems. Affirmative teams sometimes employ this same kind of strategy. They may speak as rapidly as possible in order to present a long list of need arguments. If the negative is unable to refute them all, then the "omitted ones" become the "crucial indictments" of the present system.

Such tricks and schemes should not be regarded as clever, skillful debating. Indeed, any attempt to confuse rather than to clarify the issues should be identified as unethical.

Good debaters do not need to use this kind of strategy. And if they are well prepared and alert, they do not need to fear it. Since unfair strategies are usually employed to gain a "time" advantage over the opposition, the best way to counteract them is to identify the intent of the strategy and to persist in devoting time to the major issues. Debaters who ask many questions or present trivial arguments should be challenged to show the significance of their questions and arguments. Debaters who have prepared their cases carefully and presented them effectively do not need to worry about the strategy of the opposition. They will have sound cases that can be defended by skillful refutation and rebuttal.

Programed test

1. First question: A skillful debater will refute every argument and every item of proof.
    If true, go to item 15.
    If false, go to item 11.
2. Correct. Next question: You can evaluate the worth of an opinion by evaluating the magazine, newspaper, etc., in which it is published.
    If true, go to item 10.
    If false, go to item 14.
3. The statement is not false, because the refutation of major arguments is vital to competitive debate. As arguments worthy of an answer are presented, it is the obligation of the opposition to fulfill its burden of rebuttal and to answer these arguments.
    Return to item 13.
4. Correct. Next question: When reasoning from example or analogy, you should not mention exceptions to your conclusion.
    If true, go to item 17.
    If false, go to item 13.

5. The statement is not true, because attacking an opponent's case is only *one* use of refutation. Refutation is also used to defend one's own case.

Return to item 16.

6. Correct. Next question: A skillful debater will use strategy effectively.

If true, go to item 12.

If false, go to item 16.

7. Correct. You have completed the programed test for Chapter 5.

8. The statement is not true, because counter-evidence may only produce a stalemate; the best way to refute evidence is to determine whether it actually proves what the opposition says it does.

Return to item 11.

9. The statement is not true, because a large number of examples may simply reveal the same information from the same sources; the most important question is: Are the examples typical or representative? If the examples are not typical, the generalization may be built on isolated or unique occurrences.

Return to item 14.

10. The statement is not true, because authorities do not limit their writings to certain specific sources. Although some magazines, newspapers, etc., are usually better than others, any source may publish the views of an expert.

Return to item 2.

11. Correct. Next question: The best way to refute the evidence of the opposition is to present evidence that supports an opposite point of view.

If true, go to item 8.

If false, go to item 2.

12. The statement is not true, because a skillful debater will be most effective by *not* using strategy at all; his first obligation is to the logical requirements of his case. The use of strategy to gain an unfair advantage should not be identified as skillful debating.

Return to item 6.

13. Correct. Next question: Unless major arguments are carried forward with attack or defense, a team is not accepting its burden of rebuttal.

If true, go to item 6.

If false, go to item 3.

14. Correct. Next question: The most important question for testing reasoning from example is: Have a sufficient number of examples been presented?

If true, go to item 9.
If false, go to item 4.

15. The statement is not true, because a skillful debater will want to place major emphasis on major arguments; spending time on arguments that have little or no significance may harm his attack against or his defense of vital arguments.

Return to item 1.

16. Correct. Next question: The principal use of refutation is to attack the opponent's case.

If true, go to item 5.
If false, go to item 7.

17. The statement is not true, because exceptions to a generalization or analogy should be placed in their proper perspective. Mentioning them along with other appropriate tests of reasoning will reveal the extent of their significance and actually strengthen one's case.

Return to item 4.

Exercise

Read the following statements that were presented in the 1956 presidential campaign, and arrange them in a logical order by writing the identifying letters in the appropriate blanks. The first two blanks have been filled in correctly. Number 3 should answer number 2 (I); number 4 should answer number 3, etc.

Stevenson	*Eisenhower*
1. A.	2. I.
3.	4.
5.	6.
7.	8.
9.	10.
11.	12.
13.	14.
15.	16.

Adlai E. Stevenson

A. I regret that the administration has casually dismissed my suggestion to curtail H-bomb tests; other nations have announced their willingness to comply.

B. Eisenhower's source, which estimates the danger of radioactive fall-out, is already out of date; fall-out, especially Strontium 90, is a real danger.

C. In calling the ban a "theatrical gesture," Eisenhower has indicted churchmen and political leaders the world over, who support my proposal.

D. The Republicans have greeted my suggestions with sneers and astonishing distortions, implying that even talking about them would prejudice the nation's security.

E. The President should not insist upon foolproof, perfect answers to the problem of disarmament.

F. No "last words" can be said on this fateful subject.

G. This statement is completely irrelevant. It can be regarded only as a deliberate effort to mislead. The fact is that the amount of radioactive fall-out from a single large explosion has been and can be as much as that from 1,000 smaller bombs of the Hiroshima size. Essentially all the Strontium 90 in the stratosphere comes from H-bombs.

H. Isn't it logical to assume that the U.S. should stop testing the hydrogen bomb when fall-out from nuclear tests is dangerous to mankind?

Dwight D. Eisenhower

I. The future use and control of atomic power will not come about by any theatrical national gesture, but only by explicit and supervised international agreements.

J. I might add in passing, that a political campaign does not justify a moratorium on ordinary common sense.

K. I have done everything humanly possible and consistent with national security to control the atom; these are my last words on the subject.

L. Pope Pius favors complete and controlled disarmament. We must have secure safeguards.

M. Because Strontium 90 is a result of atomic fission, which is the basic phenomenon of smaller weapons and not the hydrogen bomb, the idea that the nation could stop sending this material into the air by curtailing the tests of only large weapons is based upon apparent unawareness of the facts.

N. I shall continue to maintain that adequate safeguards are a vital necessity. It is the opposition who is misleading you.

O. The real peril or danger lies in the opposite direction; we cannot curtail our power unless secure safeguards are achieved. We must not jeopardize the security of our nation.

P. The present rate of testing does not imperil the health of humanity, because the National Academy of Sciences has indicated that the radiation exposure from all tests to date—and from continuing tests at the same rate—is, and would be, only a small fraction of the exposure that individuals receive from natural sources and medical X rays.

Assignments

For the sample debate in Appendix A:
1. Evaluate the evidence used by each side in the debate.
2. Evaluate the reasoning used by each side in the debate.
3. Select three items of evidence or reasoning and trace their development throughout the debate.

For the proposition you will be debating:
1. Select several items of evidence and test their adequacy.
2. Select several patterns of reasoning and test their validity.
3. Prepare answers for arguments that may be used against your case.

Suggested references

Brockriede, Wayne E. "A Standard for Judging Applied Logic in Debate," *The AFA Register*, X (Spring 1962), 10–14.

Crocker, Lionel. "The Debater and His Handling of Facts," *The AFA Register*, XI (Spring 1963), 18–22.

Mazza, Joseph M., and Jerome B. Polisky. "A Macroscopic View of Rebuttal," *The AFA Register*, XI (Winter 1963), 16–19.

Newman, Robert P., and Keith R. Sanders. "A Study in the Integrity of Evidence," *The Journal of the American Forensic Association*, II (January 1965), 7–13.

The Debate: Composition and Delivery

Debate materials
Taking notes during the debate
The speeches: constructive and rebuttal
The debater as speaker
The debater as listener
Cross-examination debating

A debate lasts only an hour, but if it is a good debate, hundreds of hours have gone into its preparation. This chapter gives further suggestions for getting ready to debate, but its primary concern is the actual presentation of the debate before an audience.

Debate materials

Be sure to inventory all of your debate materials to see that they are ready for the contest. Here is a brief checklist:

1. *A well-organized file box.* During the process of developing a background of knowledge about the proposition and formulating your case, you should have accumulated a great amount of valuable information. If you have followed the suggestions in Chapter 4, you have put this material on

cards and have organized it under appropriate headings which will make your evidence easy to locate during the contest. The more material you have in books and magazines scattered around you, the more time it will take to find your evidence. A few key books or magazines are often necessary, but a well-organized file box will improve your efficiency.

2. *Transparent cellulose acetate covers.* Case outlines, lists of evils, etc., can be placed in these covers. During the debate, you can use a grease pencil to check or circle appropriate arguments, supporting evidence, etc. After the debate, you can erase the marks so that the outlines and lists can be used again for the next debate. The affirmative can use these covers for case outlines and supporting evidence. The negative can use them for constructive arguments and for a list of possible evils in the affirmative plan.

3. *A large spiral drawing pad.* A large pad is convenient for note-taking, but you should not hold it in front of you while you are speaking. Before the debate, each team should rule off four columns on such a pad (see examples on page 77). The affirmative should write a brief outline of its case in the first column. The negative should write a brief outline of its constructive arguments in the second column. During the course of the debate, you can record the arguments of the opposition and your own refutation in the appropriate columns.

4. *Small spiral pads.* Use small pads for writing notes to your colleague during the debate. Some debaters like to use a separate note pad for a record of their opponents' evidence. With this plan, their large notebook will carry a record of their opponents' main contentions; the small pad will show the quality of their opponents' supporting evidence. Most debaters, though, prefer to integrate their notes on the opposition's evidence with their notes on the opposition's case, using the one big pad for both kinds of notes.

5. *Red and blue ball point pens.* Use pens instead of pencils, because notes taken in pencil are often difficult to read. Use red ink to star or underscore important arguments or significant pieces of evidence. Some debaters like to use several colors of ink, but you should keep the color system simple. Whatever system you use should aid, not complicate, your notetaking.

Taking notes during the debate

With the large spiral pad, you can take four-column notes (see the examples on page 77). When it is time for the rebuttal speeches, you

76   should be able to trace any given argument throughout the four constructive speeches.

The notetaking process varies from team to team. Some teams divide the responsibility evenly; others follow a policy of rugged individualism, in which each team member does as he pleases. Because an academic debate is a contest between teams, one would expect the debaters to work together as teams and divide at least some of the responsibilities. The two methods that are described in the following paragraphs represent two extremes. You and your colleague should examine these extremes and decide together which of these methods or combination of methods will best suit your individual preferences.

Complete division of responsibility for notetaking—the affirmative. Before the debate, the affirmative debaters will have written down a brief outline of their case on the large spiral pad. While the first affirmative debater is speaking, the second affirmative should listen attentively. During the first negative's speech, the second affirmative should record the negative's refutation in the second column opposite the affirmative case and then should note in the third column the refutation he proposes to use against the negative. If the negative presents any constructive arguments for the present system or brings up additional evils of the proposal which the first affirmative hasn't anticipated, the second affirmative should record these on either the same or a separate pad. While the second affirmative is taking notes, the first affirmative should assemble counter-evidence and also write out any advice he may have for his colleague. This process, with the same pads being used, would be reversed when the second negative gives his constructive speech and the first negative gives his rebuttal speech—then the first affirmative would take notes on both negative speeches and the second affirmative would assemble evidence and write down advice for his colleague. And, of course, the process would reverse once more during the second negative's rebuttal speech (see the order of constructive and rebuttal speeches given in Chapter 1).

Complete division of responsibility for notetaking—the negative. The negative team can follow the same general pattern. If you are the next speaker, you can take notes and your colleague can find the evidence. Since the objections you raise or evils you predict for the affirmative proposal vary from one debate to another, you should make as complete a list as possible of "undesirable effects" and slip it inside a

Affirmative Notes

1st Aff.	1st Neg.	2nd Aff.	2nd Neg.
An outline of your case (To be typed)	Notes on negative refutation	notes on your reply	notes on negative refutation
		. . . . Your plan (To be typed)	. . . . notes on negative refutation of your plan

Negative Notes

1st Aff.	1st Neg.	2nd Aff.	2nd Neg.
notes on affirmative case	Your constructive arguments (To be typed) and notes on your refutation	notes on their reply	notes on your refutation
		. . . . notes on the affirmative plan	. . . . notes on your refutation of their plan

78 transparent cellulose acetate cover (see the checklist for debate materials, pages 74–75). While you listen to the affirmative speakers, you can circle with a grease pencil the evils that you can predict for a particular affirmative case. Your colleague can then pull out and organize the necessary evidence.

No division of responsibility for notetaking. When a "team" decides not to divide the notetaking responsibility, each debater takes his own notes and assembles his own evidence. If you do not remain with one colleague for an appreciable length of time, you may find this kind of arrangement a necessity. In such a situation, do the best you can in formulating a case that is agreeable to you both and in becoming thoroughly acquainted with the material in your colleague's file box.

The speeches: constructive and rebuttal

Organization. Although no speaker except the first affirmative can have his constructive speech completely organized in advance of the debate, both teams should have their cases carefully outlined. The negative outline, of course, will have to remain more tentative than the affirmative outline. Naturally, the members of both teams will have to organize their individual speeches as the debate proceeds, in order to answer the arguments of their opponents, as they are advanced.

In Chapters 2 and 3, suggestions were made for organizing constructive and rebuttal speeches. It would be well at this point to review those suggestions and to study carefully the format of the sample outlines. Most important is a complete acceptance of the value of logical outlining. In a sense, a debate can be viewed as two opposing outlines, one more logical than the other or built upon better evidence. The time you spend on discovering the issues, determining the contentions, and finding effective evidence and reasoning with which to support your contentions is certainly time well spent. There will be little, or no, time during the contest itself to do research. For that reason, before the debate you should review your case outline carefully and appraise its adequacy.

In a *logical outline* each subpoint is a *reason for* the previous major point. Place the word *for, because,* or *since* after a main point to test whether the subpoints under it are related to it logically. In a *topical outline,* on the other hand, each subpoint is a breakdown, an explanation, or an illustration of the previous major point. The topical outline is used to describe the affirmative's plan. In the sample outlines in Chapters 2 and 3, observe the relationships between the main points, the subpoints, the sub-subpoints, etc. Note that the affirmative case ordinarily combines logical and topical outlining, and the negative case ordinarily is all logical outlining. Notice the consistent use of symbols (I, A, 1, a, etc.), the use of parallel structure for the major points and for all the subpoints under one major point, and the use of careful coordination and subordination.

Always check each entry in your outline to be sure you have stated it as clearly and concisely as possible. It is foolish to try to confuse your opponents with complicated wording. Complicated wording will probably confuse the judge also, and, perhaps, yourselves as well. As a result, the judge will probably give you a lower rating.

If you have outlined your case carefully before the debate, you should have little trouble in organizing your individual speeches during the course of the debate. If you share notetaking responsibility with your colleague (see page 76), you will organize most of your speech as you record the opposition's remarks.

Transitions and internal summaries. In the course of your constructive and rebuttal speeches, provide frequent transitional and relational words: *In the first place, next, however, on the other hand, finally, as a result,* etc. Summarize your progress briefly as you move from one argument to another. With this kind of assistance, your audience will be better able to follow the general organization of your case and to understand the significance of your various points.

Language. Use language to make ideas clear, not to impress. Choose words that are in common usage, words that your audience can be expected to understand. If the nature of your subject requires some technical language, be sure to explain it briefly when you first use it. Ordinarily, avoid slang or any other hackneyed words and expressions that have become vague and inexact from overuse. Most debates deal with serious subjects that should be discussed in a serious way; any humorous remarks you make should certainly be appropriate to the occasion. You should always use the most precise language of which you are capable and should express your ideas in a dignified, concise manner.

A common fault among debaters is to use confusing "shortcuts." Because of the strict time limits for debate speeches, some debaters

80 condense many arguments into a brief phrase, which is often not understood by the audience. For example, a debater might say, "There is no need," when he means "There are no serious shortcomings in the present system," or "The affirmative arguments do not justify changing the present system." He sometimes uses expressions like "The affirmative need does not stand," when he means "The affirmative need arguments are not a cause for action." In your use of language, you should have absolute clarity as your major goal.

The debater as speaker

The good debater, like any other public speaker, not only must master his subject matter, organize his thoughts carefully and express them in precise, clear language, but must *deliver* his speech in a forceful, convincing manner. The following brief suggestions cannot take the place of a course in public speaking—a course from which all debaters would profit greatly. They can, though, if practiced conscientiously, help you make the best possible impression on your audience and help you present your case persuasively.

1. *Dress with dignity.* It seems pretty obvious that you should be neat and well-groomed. You will make a good impression on your audience and you will gain a certain amount of self-confidence in knowing that you look your best. Men should normally wear a suit and tie or a conservative sport coat and matching trousers. Women should dress neatly and simply and should be conservative in their use of cosmetics and jewelry.
2. *Do not rush or stall between speeches.* Give your opponents and the judge time to prepare themselves for the next speech. If you rush your audience, you may cause them to miss an essential argument. Take a moment to exchange a few brief words with your colleague and then go to the rostrum as soon as everyone seems to be ready. On the other hand, do not go to the other extreme and create an unnecessary delay.
3. *Be purposeful in movement and gesture.* The manner in which you approach and speak at the rostrum should reveal the confidence you have in your debate case. Avoid the extremes of too much or too little movement and gesture. If you are enthusiastic about your subject, your gestures will arise naturally and spontaneously. Carefully rehearsed gestures will call attention to themselves and away from what you are saying.

4. *Be alert, but at ease, in posture.* Do not drape yourself over the rostrum. Be erect, but not stiff. The audience should see an alert speaker who gives an energetic and varied presentation.

5. *Do not overuse your notes.* Even while reading evidence, maintain direct eye contact with your audience by your discreet use of notes. Use note cards rather than flimsy sheets of paper, which are likely to rattle and to distract attention.

6. *Use suitable volume, rate, and pitch.* Speak loudly enough so that everyone can hear and slowly and distinctly enough so that everyone can understand. Of particular concern in debate is the speaker's rate of delivery. Because of the strict time limits and because of the many arguments to be covered, debaters often speak much too fast. Some teams use a rapid rate of delivery as a kind of strategy by which they manage to "talk about" more arguments than the other team. A "speed case," as it is sometimes called, does not produce good public speaking, and it should not be considered good debating. It places emphasis on "covering" a good many arguments, not on determining the major arguments and discussing them thoroughly. Try to speak at your normal pitch, avoiding both a too high and a too low pitch. Vary your pitch, though; don't speak in a monotone. If you are truly interested in and enthusiastic about your subject, you probably won't have to worry about speaking in a monotonous tone of voice.

7. *Use a conversational mode of delivery.* The basic pattern of your speaking should be conversational. In most good conversation there is eagerness to communicate, direct eye contact, and a general impression of spontaneity and ease. A manner of delivery marked by display, affectation, and artfulness has no place in debate, where the emphasis should be on direct and forceful communication. Good debate delivery, like good public speaking, is *"enlarged* conversation," for it involves more volume, dignity, bodily movement, and careful articulation than ordinary conversation requires.

The debater as listener

The debate situation calls for accurate and critical listening. If you misunderstand or misinterpret your opponents, you may end up challenging evidence they did not present or refuting arguments they did not advance. And this is a sure way to lose a debate. If you follow the suggestions for dividing responsibilities with your colleague, you

82   should develop a pattern for efficient notetaking. These three additional suggestions will help you further improve your listening
effectiveness:

1. *Talk between, not during, speeches.* It is not only poor manners to
   talk when your opponents are speaking, but it is also folly, because you will hear only part of the opposition's presentation.
   While you are talking, you may miss some argument or evidence
   that is vital to the debate. Listen carefully to your opponents.
   Unless you understand their position, you cannot expect to refute
   it.
2. *Write notes to your colleague.* If you want to remind your colleague
   about some evidence or possible refutation, write him a note. You
   can select the appropriate time to write it, and he can select the
   appropriate time to read it. One of you should always be listening
   to the opposition's presentation.
3. *Show proper respect for the opposition.* Do not reveal your attitudes
   toward your opponents or toward their case by facial expressions
   or head movements that indicate disagreement or displeasure. Be
   courteous and fair-minded. An attitude of quiet confidence is
   preferred to one of loud arrogance. You should try to be identified
   as a friendly person who conducts himself in a sensible, dignified
   manner.

Cross-examination debating

As we learned in Chapter 5, the strongest possible foundation from
which to attack an opponent's case or to defend your own case is a
thorough analysis of the proposition culminating in a strong affirmative or negative case. In cross-examination debating, where each
constructive speech is followed by a question period,[2] the direct clash
of attack and defense dramatizes the contrasts between the two
teams. A debater can use the question period to elicit information
which can clarify the issues, to test the analysis and proof of the
opposition, and to lay the groundwork for the development of his
own case. This section will present some principles and suggestions
for participating in cross-examination debating.

Principles for both teams. If the question periods are to aid rather
than hinder the debate process, then both teams should adhere to
certain principles:

2. See Chapter 1, pages 9–10, for a suggested pattern of speaking order and time limits.

1. Participants should be courteous, reasonable, and cooperative with a willingness to deal with the essential issues. Discourtesy, unreasonableness, uncooperativeness, and unwillingness to deal with the essential issues are all marks of poor debating. Do not browbeat your opponent, and do not be sarcastic.
2. Remember that all phases of the actual contest involve public speaking. Although you are questioning only one person, be sure to speak so that the audience can understand your questions, too. The witness should also address the audience as well as the questioner.
3. During the question period, neither speaker may confer with his colleague. Each one is on his own.
4. Both questions and answers should be brief. Avoid complex and negative questions, and make little use of the phrase, "Isn't it a fact that. . . ." Although a questioner cannot require all "yes" or "no" answers, he need not tolerate stalling tactics, and the witness need not tolerate long speeches by the questioner. Remember, though, that all disagreements must be presented in a courteous and reasonable manner.

Suggestions for the questioner. These are not rules, but ideas for making your presentation more effective.

1. Plan a *series* of questions in advance. Place them in a transparent cover; circle with a grease pencil those questions that are most appropriate for the opposition's case. Begin with common ground or admitted matter and then proceed to areas of disagreement. The questions, presented in Chapter 5, for testing evidence and reasoning can provide a helpful beginning, but they must be adapted to each case. Do not jump from point to point.
2. Use the information revealed in the question period in your constructive and rebuttal speeches. Confine your cross-examination time to questions. This time is not intended for the presentation of additional evidence or constructive material; neither is it the time to argue with your opponent. Do not press for final admissions of faulty analysis or weak evidence; use your regular speaking time to draw these conclusions.
3. Although you cannot know how the opposition will answer all of your questions, you should be reasonably sure of the possible answers and what you intend to make of them. Unexpected answers to crucial questions may cause obvious embarrassment to you.

84 4. Use a summary question to conclude each series; it will provide an obvious conclusion to one series and prepare the audience for another. Sometimes the original opening question can be used: "Do you still believe that. . . ." or "Is it still your position that. . . ."

Suggestions for the witness. These suggestions should sharpen your ability to respond effectively.

1. Be prepared for the kinds of questions that might be raised about your case, and plan your answers. The question period should not be full of surprises for you.
2. In answering, be as direct and fair as possible. If you must qualify an answer, do so briefly. It is better to admit lack of knowledge of certain facts, than to allow the questioner to reveal your obvious evasions. Careful preparation should equip you with all significant facts. Whether you should know certain obscure facts must be left up to the audience and the judge.
3. You may refuse to answer an unfair question, but your reason for doing so should be explained briefly.
4. Do not try to cross-examine the questioner. It is not good debating and is a sign of an inexperienced debater.

• If you have mastered the subject matter, organized your case carefully, practiced refutation and rebuttal speeches, and developed an effective delivery, you are prepared for the debate contest.

Programed test

1. First question: The traditional negative case combines logical and topical outlining.
    If true, go to item 12.
    If false, go to item 17.
2. The statement is true, because each team tries to formulate a logical statement in support of its position. Outlining one's case is an excellent way to establish the logical relationships between its various elements. A comparison of the outlines can reveal the relative strength of the opposing cases.
    Return to item 15.
3. Correct. Next question: A good debater will try to talk about

more arguments than his opponent does.

If true, go to item 16.

If false, go to item 10.

4.   The statement is not true, because a debater should be quietly confident of his case. The time to be responsive and to reveal one's reactions is during his own constructive and rebuttal speeches.

Return to item 10.

5.   The statement is not true, because bodily movement should not be characterized by display. Such movement would call attention to itself and diminish communication.

Return to item 14.

6.   Correct. Next question: Composition ends when one's case is completed and delivery begins.

If true, go to item 13.

If false, go to item 15.

7.   Correct. Next question: One objective of the question period in cross-examination debating is to discredit your opponent and his arguments.

If true, go to item 11.

If false, go to item 14.

8.   The statement is true, because a few key books or magazines can be used during the debate to investigate briefly an argument a debate team did not think the opposition would present.

Return to item 17.

9.   Correct. You have completed the programed test for Chapter 6.

10. Correct. Next question: A debater should be responsive and show his reactions to the opposition's case as it is being presented.

If true, go to item 4.

If false, go to item 9.

11. The statement is not true, because attempting to discredit your opponent is not a sign of courteous, reasonable behavior. Deal in issues rather than personalities.

Return to item 7.

12. The statement is not true, because the traditional negative case contains all logical outlining. Some topical outlining would probably be used in the plan description of a counter-plan case.

Return to item 1.

13. The statement is not true, because debaters must compose their speeches during the debate. Each debate has unique combinations of argument and evidence.

Return to item 6.

14. Correct. Next question: Public speaking is enlarged conversation,

because it usually involves more dignity and display of bodily movement.

> *If true, go to item 5.*
> *If false, go to item 3.*

15. Correct. Next question: A debate contest can be viewed as two opposing outlines — the outline of the affirmative case and the outline of the negative case.

> *If true, go to item 7.*
> *If false, go to item 2.*

16. The statement is not true, because the total number of arguments treated is not nearly so important as the number of arguments that are particularly significant in the debate. A good debater will devote most of his time to the significant contentions and the evidence and reasoning used to support them.

> *Return to item 3.*

17. Correct. Next question: Debaters should select a few key books or magazines and have them ready for use during the debate.

> *If true, go to item 6.*
> *If false, go to item 8.*

Exercise

Using the skeleton outline, arrange the following statements in the logical order of a traditional affirmative case.[3] Be sure to add the appropriate transitions (i.e., "for" or "and") where they are needed.

End the draft as soon as it is consistent with national security.

It doesn't provide the incentives for quality men to make the service a career.

Significant benefits will result from the affirmative plan.

About 750,000 men, some of high quality, will leave the armed forces in 1956.

The draft is not meeting our military needs.

There is a need for a change.

Our armed forces would be strengthened.

Strengthen the incentives for a military career.

The affirmative proposes the following plan.

Experienced and professional personnel would be retained in the military.

Our military system is inefficient and costly.

---

3. The case is based upon real arguments presented by Adlai E. Stevenson in various speeches, written statements, and news conferences of the 1956 presidential campaign.

It doesn't supply the experienced personnel needed for modern weapons.

We could meet our needs on a voluntary basis.

The government will spend $2,500,000,000 for the basic training of replacements alone.

Resolved: That the selective service policies of the U.S. should be re-examined.

I.

    A.

        1.

        2.

    B.

        1.

        2.

II.

    A.

    B.

III.

    A.

        1.

    B.

For the sample debate in Appendix A:
1. Prepare a set of four column notes on the debate.
2. Describe and evaluate the transitions used by the debaters.
3. Evaluate the language used in the debate.

For the proposition you will be debating:
1. Inventory your debate materials and prepare them for an actual debate.
2. Be prepared to deliver an extemporaneous speech on your constructive arguments.
3. Be prepared to refute orally various arguments that will be presented by the opposition.

Suggested references

Cathcart, Robert S. "Adapting Debate to an Audience," *The Speech Teacher*, V (March 1956), 113–116.

Christopherson, Merrill G. "The Necessity for Style in Argument," *The Speech Teacher*, IX (March 1960), 116–120.

Freshley, Dwight L. "A Case for More Cross-Examination Debating," *The Journal of The American Forensic Association*, II (January 1965), 21–24.

Friedman, Robert P. "Why Not Debate Persuasively?" *Today's Speech*, V (January 1957), 32–34.

Fuge, Lloyd H., and Robert P. Newman. "Cross-Examination in Academic Debating," *The Speech Teacher*, V (January 1956), 66–70.

Hance, Kenneth G. "The Concept of Ethical Proof in Persuasion and Debate," *The AFA Register*, VI (Spring 1958), 5–12.

Klopf, Donald, and James C. McCroskey. "Ethical Practices in Debate," *The Journal of the American Forensic Association*, I (January 1964), 13–16.

McBath, James H., and Nicholas M. Cripe. "Delivery: Rhetoric's Rusty Canon," *The Journal of the American Forensic Association*, II (January 1965), 1–6.

Judging
a
Debate

Professional differences in judging
Standards for judging debates
Sample ballots
Receiving a decision

After a debate, a decision is given. Sometimes, when two teams are pretty evenly matched, evaluation is very difficult, and the decision, regardless of how carefully considered it is, will not satisfy everyone. Even experienced, impartial judges may disagree about a decision. Familiarity with professional differences in judging, with the various standards for judging, and with the different kinds of ballots can help you to understand decisions, even though you may not always agree with them. As a debater, you can make use of the judge's decision in at least two ways: (1) From it, you can gain insight into the virtues and faults of your performance so that you can improve your subsequent debating. (2) By trying to understand the

90 judge's methods and the reasoning behind his decisions, you can gain skill in your own judging of debates.

Most people agree that participation in academic debate is justified because of the training it gives in research, critical thinking, argument, and extemporaneous speaking. Debate experience should also include practice in judging debates. If you cannot evaluate your own performance and the performance of others, you have not completed your training in debate.

Professional differences in judging

If you have some knowledge of the many variable factors in a debate and of the differing criteria judges use in making decisions, you should be able to understand why judges often disagree. But regardless of general agreement on basic principles, primarily those explained in Chapter 1, a judge cannot escape some subjectivity in the many evaluations he is forced to make — Has the affirmative really presented a prima facie case? How sound are its reasoning and evidence? Must an affirmative team win all the issues in order to be judged the better team? Has the negative team done the better debating if it concentrates on and defeats one issue? The answers to the last two questions crystallize the differences between *logical* and *proficiency* decisions.

Logical decisions. Some judges render a decision on the basis of which team has "won" on the issues. Since issues are defined as *vital* and inherent questions on which the outcome of the debate hinges, the judge who gives a logical decision will vote for an affirmative team only if it has won *all* the issues. Otherwise, the judge will vote for the negative, even if the negative attack has been limited to only one issue. If, in the opinion of the judge, the affirmative team has not presented a prima facie case, he will vote for the negative team, even though the negative may be extremely incompetent. The judge will award the negative the decision merely on the basis of its presumption.

The greatest justification in giving a "logical decision" is that it is based on and consistent with the concepts of burden of proof, presumption, burden of rebuttal, and the role of issues in a debate. The greatest weakness is that it is an absolute rather than a comparative decision. For example, if the judge believes that the affirmative has not presented a prima facie case, he will vote for the negative because of its presumption; as a matter of fact, the judge could vote for the negative team even before it speaks. Depending upon your point of view, you might say that the affirmative has defeated itself, or that the judge has "won" the debate against the affirmative.

Proficiency decisions. A proficiency decision is based upon the quality of debating done by each team. The debate, it is assumed, is held not to settle questions of fact, value, or policy, but to decide which of the two teams has shown the greater skill in debate. Therefore, an affirmative team which has lost a crucial contention may still be awarded the decision on the basis of its overall superior handling of analysis, evidence, refutation, and delivery. The greatest strength of a proficiency decision is that it is comparative. The judge must hear all speakers before he can give a decision. The greatest weakness of a proficiency decision is that it may be inconsistent with debate theory; the negative may win an issue but lose the debate.

These two approaches to judging do not come into conflict so long as teams of similar ability are debating. If the quality of debating done by both teams is about the same, the judge will then turn to specific issues and contentions. Furthermore, a team that cannot create a prima facie case is very likely to be the poorer team. However, in the opinion of the author, the *decision should be comparative.* If the negative does not recognize the deficiencies in the affirmative case, then the question remains: Which team did the better debating? The decision will have to be made on aspects of the contest other than the affirmative's failure to create a prima facie case or the negative's inability to recognize this failure. In other words, the judge's decision should be based upon the comparative proficiency of the debaters.

Standards for judging debates

The most important thing for all judges to remember is that *the decision is comparative. Two* teams are debating. If the affirmative team uses poor evidence, but the negative team does not challenge the evidence, then neither team recognizes poor evidence, and the decision cannot be against the affirmative merely because of its inferior evidence. If the negative team has weaknesses in its attack, but the affirmative does not detect them, then the negative team can be criticized for poor analysis or refutation and the affirmative team can be criticized for poor counter-refutation. Consequently, the decision must be based on other factors, factors which will show a

AFFIRMATIVE

Round No._____   Room No._____   Judge No._____

Assign to each speaker the number which best describes the quality of his debating. The team with the highest total should be declared the winner.

	Poor	Fair	Good	Excellent	Superior	
#	3-4	5-6-7	8-9-10	11-12-13	14-15	#

Aff. Team_____   Neg. Team_____

1st Aff._____ # _____   1st Neg._____ # _____

2nd Aff._____ # _____   2nd Neg._____ # _____

Total _____   Total _____

In my opinion, the better debating was done by_____ _____
                                                                        No.   School   Side

1st Aff.   2nd Aff.

Rebuttal   Rebuttal

Signed_____
                      Judge

Figure 1

This form has been used at Bowling Green State University.

NEGATIVE

Round No._____   Room No._____   Judge No._____

Assign to each speaker the number which best describes the quality of his debating. The team with the highest total should be declared the winner.

	Poor	Fair	Good	Excellent	Superior	
#	3-4	5-6-7	8-9-10	11-12-13	14-15	#

Aff. Team_____   Neg. Team_____

   1st Aff._____ # _____   1st Neg._____ # _____

   2nd Aff._____ # _____   2nd Neg._____ # _____

              Total _____   Total _____

In my opinion, the better debating was done by _____ _____
                                                    No.   School   Side

1st Neg.

2nd Neg.

Rebuttal

Rebuttal

Signed_____
              Judge

Figure 2

This form has been used at Bowling Green State University.

American Forensic Association Debate Ballot

FORM **C**

Division_____ Round_____ Room_____ Date_____ Judge_____

Affirmative_____ Negative_____

Check the column on each item which, on the following scale, best describes your evaluation of the speaker's effectiveness:

1—poor	2—fair	3—average	4—excellent	5—superior

1st Affirmative						2nd Affirmative							1st Negative						2nd Negative				
1	2	3	4	5		1	2	3	4	5			1	2	3	4	5		1	2	3	4	5
												Analysis											
												Reasoning											
												Evidence											
												Organization											
												Refutation											
												Delivery											

Total_____ Total_____ Total_____ Total_____

Team Ratings: AFFIRMATIVE: poor   fair   average   excellent   superior
NEGATIVE: poor   fair   average   excellent   superior

Rank each debater in order of excellence (1st for best, 2nd for next best, etc.).

COMMENTS: COMMENTS:
1st Aff. (name)_____Rank ( )   1st Neg. (name)_____Rank ( )

2nd Aff. (name)_____Rank ( )   2nd Neg. (name)_____Rank ( )

In my opinion, the better debating was done by the_____
                                                    (AFFIRMATIVE OR NEGATIVE)

_____   _____
JUDGE'S SIGNATURE   SCHOOL

Figure 3

Form C has been reprinted by permission of the American Forensic Association.

American Forensic Association Debate Ballot

FORM **D**

Division.................... Round.................... Room.................... Date.................... Judge....................

Affirmative.. Negative....................

INSTRUCTIONS

Rank the debaters in their order of excellence: 1 for best, 2 for second best, etc.

Rate the effectiveness of each debater in a manner similar to the way you grade in school; i.e., A, B, C, etc. However, on the ballot use rating points as indicated by the following table:

A + $=$15; A$=$14; A $-$ $=$13; B $+$ $=$12; B$=$11; B $-$ $=$10; C $+$ $=$9; C$=$8; C $-$ $=$7;

D $+$ $=$6; D$=$5; D $-$ $=$4; E $+$ $=$3; E$=$2; E $-$ $=$1.

Name	Rank	Rating points
1st Affirmative		
2nd Affirmative		
1st Negative		
2nd Negative		

(NOTE: Rank and Rating points should correlate with the decision; i.e., the winning team should receive the higher total in rating points and get the lower total in ranking. In close debates the rank might be tied but the rating points should favor the winning team.)

COMMENTS:
1st Aff.:

COMMENTS:
1st Neg.:

2nd Aff.:

2nd Neg.:

In my opinion, the better debating was done by the ....

(AFFIRMATIVE OR NEGATIVE)

JUDGE'S SIGNATURE   SCHOOL

Figure 4

Form D has been reprinted by permission of the American Forensic Association.

96   difference between the two teams. It would seem that a fair decision could be made if the two teams could be compared as to their handling of each of the following four items:

1. *Analysis.* Evaluate the reasoning the debater used to construct his case.
2. *Evidence.* Evaluate the facts and opinions the debater used to support his reasoning.
3. *Refutation.* Evaluate the debater's ability to destroy opposing proofs and to defend his own.
4. *Delivery.* Evaluate the debater's skill in public speaking.

In a close debate, one of these items may become crucial; the decision may even rest on the refutation of one contention. It is unrealistic to insist that the judge give a numerical rating to each of the above items and then total them to determine the winner; this procedure assumes that the various items are always of equal importance, and that is simply not true. Although it is easy to make a score reflect the desired outcome, a judge should be expected only to indicate a "winner" and to assign a quality rating or a point rating to indicate superior, excellent, good, fair, or poor debating. A judge should always indicate on the ballot why he voted the way he did.

Sample ballots

Study the ballots given on pages 92–95. Note that the first two ballots (see Figures 1 and 2) reflect the judging standards just described. Both ballots require the judge to assign an overall quality rating to each debater, and both ballots provide that the winning team must receive the higher points, which would be indicative of its overall proficiency. The third ballot (see Figure 3) requires the judge to assign each debater points on six separate items. Such ballots, of course, can show specific strengths and weaknesses in a team's debating skill.

Receiving a decision

Regardless of your feeling about the decision, accept it with good grace — as a winner or a loser. Even though you receive a "wrong" decision, there is no point in disputing it. Let the audience do the complaining, if complaints are justified. Courtesy is just as important after the debate as it is during the debate. It will probably be difficult, if not impossible, at the end of the debate to receive the decision with complete detachment. The truth is, though, that the values of educational debate are far more important than the victories you may win or the defeats you may suffer. There is no question, however, that victory is exhilarating, and you should strive for it by preparing the best case of which you are capable and presenting your case and refuting that of your opponents to the best of your ability.

• The best way to achieve skill in evaluating debate is to seize every opportunity to practice judging debates. Devise a ballot similar to one of those given on pages 92–95. Compare your decision with the one reached by your coach or the judge. If, as many people think, the main objective of competitive debate is to increase a student's ability to formulate and present competitive ideas, then he should also be able to appraise his own progress toward that goal. Judging debates can help provide the necessary criteria for evaluation.

Programed test

1. First question: Educational debates are held to settle questions of fact, value, or policy.
    If true, go to item 10.
    If false, go to item 16.
2. The statement is true, because a judge giving a logical decision may vote for the negative even if he has not heard the negative speakers. Obviously, this is not a comparative decision. Thus, the judge's evaluation is absolute, for he decides who has "won" the issues and votes accordingly.
    Return to item 14.
3. Correct. Next question: In a logical decision, a negative team can win merely on the strength of its presumption.
    If true, go to item 14.
    If false, go to item 17.
4. Correct. You have completed the programed test for Chapter 7.
5. The statement is true, because a judge is forced to make many subjective evaluations. Considering eight speeches and four speakers, he has to decide which team has the better analysis, evidence, refutation, and delivery.
    Return to item 12.

98   6. Correct. Next question: A proficiency decision may rest on which team wins one specific issue.

If true, go to item 12.

If false, go to item 15.

7.   The statement is true, because a judge will render a logical decision if the teams have the same proficiency; thus, the two methods of judging would merge.

Return to item 11.

8.   The statement is not true, because an affirmative team may lose an issue and still win on the basis of its overall proficiency. It is the logical decision which is consistent with the theoretical principles of debate.

Return to item 16.

9.   Correct. Next question: In a logical decision, an affirmative debater can lose one issue and still win the debate.

If true, go to item 13.

If false, go to item 11.

10. The statement is not true, because an educational debate is held to decide which team has the greater skill in debate. Therefore, the convictions of the judge should not enter into his final evaluation of which team did the better debating.

Return to item 1.

11. Correct. Next question: If two teams are virtually the same in debating ability and skill, then conflict between a logical or proficiency decision is not likely to occur.

If true, go to item 4.

If false, go to item 7.

12. Correct. Next question: It is relatively easy to understand why judges often disagree.

If true, go to item 9.

If false, go to item 5.

13. The statement is not true, because a logical decision adheres strictly to the logical obligations of the affirmative debater; therefore, failing to carry one issue means losing the debate.

Return to item 9.

14. Correct. Next question: A logical decision is an absolute rather than a comparative decision.

If true, go to item 6.

If false, go to item 2.

15. The statement is not false, because two teams may be virtually the same in debating skill; then, the judge may have to look to a single issue.

Return to item 6.

16. Correct. Next question: The greatest strength of a proficiency decision is that it is consistent with the principles of debate explained in Chapter 1.

If true, go to item 8.

If false, go to item 3.

17. The statement is not false, because a logical decision for the affirmative debaters requires that they present a prima facie case. If the affirmative case is not prima facie, the logical decision would automatically be for the negative, because of the negative's presumption.

Return to item 3.

Exercise

Read the following statements that might be made by debate judges. Identify the comments as representative of logical (L) or proficiency (P) decisions.

Decision   *Statement*

_____1. The affirmative did not present a prima facie case, and so my vote for the negative is really no more than a vote against the affirmative.

_____2. Delivery was a very important factor in this particular debate; the affirmative debaters were definitely the better speakers.

_____3. Granted that the negative attack was most decisive, I still doubt that it is good debating to deal with only one stock issue.

_____4. Technically, I think the affirmative lost this debate, but I voted for them, because, considering all factors, I think they will represent our region in the national tournament better than the negative team could.

_____5. The word "negative" should appear on every ballot when the affirmative does not establish a prima facie case.

_____6. This was a very close debate; I had difficulty weighing the differences between the two teams.

_____7. I know that the negative was quite incompetent, but the affirmative did not give an adequate answer to a crucial negative question.

_____8. The affirmative team did not refute the obvious weaknesses in negative proof, and so I had to look to other factors in reaching my decision.

100   *Assignments*

For the sample debate in Appendix A:
1. Use one of the sample debate ballots to evaluate the debate. Omitting an evaluation of delivery, decide which team did the better debating. Explain your answer.
2. Prepare an oral defense for your decision.

For the proposition you will be debating:
1. Use one of the sample debate ballots to evaluate a classroom scrimmage or interscholastic debate.
2. Prepare an oral defense for your decision.

Suggested references

Barker, Larry L. "A Comparative Analysis of Debater-Judge Ratings," *The Journal of the American Forensic Association,* II (January 1965), 17–20.

Clark, William K. "Debate Judging: Implications of the James Study," *The AFA Register,* IX (Convention Issue 1961), 1–5.

Drum, Dale D. "The Debate Judge as a Machine," *Today's Speech,* IV (April 1956), 28–31.

James, Herbert L. "Standards for Judging Refutation," *The AFA Register,* IX (Spring 1961), 21–25.

Kruger, Arthur N. "The Debate Judge as a Critical Thinker," *Today's Speech,* V (January 1957), 29–31.

McCroskey, James C., and Leon R. Camp. "A Study of Stock Issues, Judging Criteria, and Decisions in Debate," *The Southern Speech Journal,* XXX (Winter 1964), 158–168.

Ojala, Dorothy, and Fred Shinnick. "The Debaters' Bill of Rights," *The Speech Teacher,* IV (March 1955), 98–100.

Roever, James, and Kim Giffin. "A Study of the Use of Judging Criteria in Tournament Debate," *The AFA Register,* VII (College Calendar Issue 1959), 12–14.

Weiss, Robert O. "Judgment and Decision-Making," *The Journal of the American Forensic Association,* I (May 1964), 43–47.

The following debate[1] was the championship debate of the Fifteenth Annual National Debate Tournament, held at West Point, New York, on April 29, 1961.

The proposition was:

Resolved: That the United States should adopt a program of compulsory health insurance for all citizens.

The affirmative team: Gene Clements and Laurence Tribe, Harvard University.
The negative team: Frank Harrison and Peter Smith, Kings College.

First affirmative constructive speech: GENE CLEMENTS.

Ladies and gentlemen, because Larry and I feel that the dollar sign has no place in medicine, we're resolved: "That the United States should adopt a program of compulsory health insurance for all citizens," a program of spreading the risk of medical expense throughout society, "compulsory" in the sense that it would be financed through federal taxes. Now, in this first speech, we'd like to show you that there's a compelling need for a change, that a program of compulsory health insurance could meet that need, and that such a program would be beneficial to the American people.

Turning first to the need for a change, Larry and I will present three contentions: number one, the neglect of health is today causing needless death and suffering; number two, the primary reason for this neglect of health is that people are led to make medical decisions on economic grounds; number three, this problem is inherent in the present system.

First, then, we contend that the neglect of health is today causing needless death and suffering. The Conference on the General Welfare reported in 1959: "Due to inadequate medical care, over a third of a million lives are needlessly lost each year." Frankly, Larry and I are appalled by such a tragic waste of human life, but, of course, the problem extends far beyond those who die to the many more who suffer without the care they need. U.S. Public Health Service reported, "Last year 49.9 per cent of all acute disabling medical conditions received no medical attention whatsoever." And that this neglect endangers the health of every one of us, was pointed out by the *Public Health Reports* last February when they said, "Eight hundred thousand Americans with serious contagious diseases need medical supervision to protect the health of the general public." But 400,000 of these, that's one half, are receiving no medical supervision of any kind. The Conference on the General

---

1 The debate was transcribed from a tape recording. Permission to print it was granted by the United States Military Academy and the debaters. The affirmative team, representing Harvard University, was judged the winner by a vote of four to three.

102 Welfare pretty well sums up the situation when it says, "The health needs of the nation are grossly neglected."

The question, then, is *why?* And that's our second point. The primary reason for this neglect of health is that people are led to make medical decisions on economic grounds. In other words, in seeking medical care, all of us have to ask ourselves, "How will the bill be paid?" Our first point here is that many people just can't pay it. Professor A. F. Wessen of Washington University wrote last December, "Families are often forced to decide against seeking care that they desperately need because of the high cost of necessary medical services." Professor B. J. Stern of Columbia was a little bit more explicit when he wrote in *The Sociology of Medicine,* 1960, "For the vast majority of the people, adequate medical care has grown increasingly beyond reach because of its cost." And Professor Strauss of Columbia wrote last July, "The result of such high cost is that many health needs are neglected."

Our second point is that for still more people, even if they can pay *some* medical bills, uncertainty as to what the ultimate cost will be leads them to postpone the care or to forego it entirely. This point is substantiated by Professor of Sociology E. L. Kuhs when he says, "The possible cost of treatment — if more serious disease is later discovered — must remain an unknown factor and this uncertainty often determines whether to seek care in the first place."

Our third point is that for all of us, even if we can pay all the medical bills, the economic deterrent remains, because although we know that diagnosis and early treatment are necessary, we just may not *feel* sick; so we decide to economize by avoiding care. As Jerome Rothenberg said in the *American Economic Review,* "Consumers tend to economize by seeking medical attention only when they feel very ill, discouraging early diagnosis and treatment." In other words, because we must all make economic decisions in seeking medical care, we often postpone in the hope that our symptoms will just go away. Sometimes they don't.

We conclude then that the primary reason for the neglect of health is that people are led to make medical decisions on economic grounds. We must always ask, "How will the bill be paid?" No matter what mechanism of the present system we try to rely on, this question still remains. And that's our third point. This problem is inherent in the present system because, as Professor of Economics B. A. Weisbrod pointed out last June, "No voluntary system can remove the need to make economic decisions in seeking medical care. In self-financing, where the cost of care is directly a factor, of course, this defect is obvious. But even voluntary insurance suffers from the same inherent problem."

First, as Professor Haverman wrote last month, "Nobody can afford all the insurance he needs, and in deciding which of life's risks to brave, most individuals decide to take a chance on the family's health." And that's not too difficult to understand when you realize, as did Professor Stern of Columbia, "Even the better voluntary prepayment plans offer too little and cost too much to be included in the budgets of the majority of the population." In short, you still have to ask, "How will the bill be paid?"

Second, as *Public Health Reports* observed in June 1959, "Even when people decide to pay the premiums for some kind of insurance policy, the economic factor remains, because the amount of coverage they can buy depends, of course, on how much money they have." That's why we say that the problem is inherent in any voluntary system of medical financing. There is thus a compelling need to combat the unnecessary death and suffering in the United States. The program we adopt must be universal, since everyone is faced by economic decisions in seeking medical care. And it must be compulsory because no voluntary method of financing removes the need to make those economic decisions.

The plan we advocate is basically pretty simple: All medical bills would be sent to local boards composed of doctors and representatives of the public. These boards would set the fees, control abuses, and send cumulative bills to the Department of Health, Education, and Welfare, which would pay them out of an insurance fund financed through compulsory taxes. It would be run just like any other insurance program except that the premiums would be based on the ability to pay, and the benefits would be comprehensive, covering the diagnosis, cure, medication, treatment, or prevention of disease. Unlike the present system, the affirmative plan, by making insurance compulsory for all citizens, eliminates the need to make economic decisions in seeking medical care, for a compulsory tax based on financial ability has prepaid it. Our plan thus meets the need by freeing the American people to decide whether to get medical care on the basis of whether or not they need it.

Finally, Larry and I think that our plan could accomplish something really constructive in addition to meeting the need, and we'd like to present the major advantages of our plan right now so that the negative team will be able to consider them right from the beginning of the debate. Our first advantage is that compulsory health insurance would prevent medical cost from causing severe economic hardship. Now, the logical way to prevent an expense from causing financial hardship is, of course, to distribute that expense on the basis of financial ability, and that's exactly what compulsory health insurance would do through a progressive tax mechanism. Under the present system, any one of us might some day be struck by a financially crippling illness. In fact, Professor J. H. Richardson of the University of Leeds wrote last year, "There is conclusive quantitative evidence that a major cause of financial hardship and even poverty in the United States is heavy expenditure for medical care." Compulsory health insurance has a very real advantage here. If we remove the dollar sign from medicine, the cost of illness will no longer be allowed to transform medical tragedy into financial disaster.

Our second advantage is that compulsory health insurance would relieve the financial drain on our hospitals. Edward T. Chase pointed out in last May's *Reporter*, "The indigent often do without the care they need, to avoid receiving medical charity, but when they do accept that charity it often happens that nobody pays the bill, and then the hospitals are in serious trouble." Dr. J. P. Dixon testified in Congress in July 1959, "Unpaid bills

104 have become such a drain on resources that the quality and availability of hospital services are seriously threatened. Many of our hospitals are on the brink of financial disaster." By paying those bills through compulsory health insurance, we could eliminate this crisis before it cripples our hospitals.

Our third advantage is that compulsory health insurance would provide adequate medical care to many who must now rely on inadequate welfare services. In fact, our plan would completely eliminate second-class citizenship from medicine by providing care on an equal basis to all as a matter of right. But reviewing the present system, the Advisory Council on Public Assistance disclosed last February, "There are glaring defects in the ways the medical needs of the indigent are being met." Less than half the states fully meet welfare needs by even their own minimal standards. For those millions who must now rely on "poor man's medicine," then, compulsory health insurance provides something which the present system has failed to provide — medical equality. The affirmative plan, then, would relieve economic insecurity; it would prevent hospital insolvency; it would remove medical inequality.

In every one of these areas there's a pressing need for action. Some suggestions have been made. Perhaps the negative team may even make some here today. That's why we don't claim that these are needs in the debate sense for the affirmative resolution. But the advantage of that affirmative program is that it strikes at the heart of each one of these problems by removing economic considerations from medicine. And you remember why we must adopt such a program. We must adopt it because a third of a million lives are needlessly lost each year; because half of all the disabling acute illnesses remain untreated; because 400,000 contagious disease carriers receive no medical supervision. And all of this primarily because people must ask themselves, "How will we pay the bill?" — a question that neither they nor the present system can answer. Compulsory health insurance answers that question by removing the dollar sign from medicine.

First negative constructive speech: FRANK HARRISON.

Mr. Chairman, distinguished guests, ladies and gentlemen, I might begin by paraphrasing Winston Churchill, "Never have so many things been found so wrong with so little in so short a time." Keeping that in mind, I'd like to analyze the proposition presented to you by the gentlemen of the affirmative in somewhat of a reverse order. That is, I'd like to turn first to this question of these additional advantages. Now I think it very interesting that the first affirmative speaker told you these are not "needs" — they are just additional advantages — sort of "bonus points" that come along with the affirmative resolution. We're going to suggest that each one of them, when looked at in a more realistic light, becomes a distinct disadvantage which the affirmative will have to cope with before it can substantiate the desirability of this plan.

First, you were told it's going to prevent hardship on the part of individuals. Now we're going to ask the gentlemen of the affirmative, "Since when did it become the duty of the federal government to make sure that no person in the United States undergoes financial hardship?" If a person's home burns down, this is a tragedy. If his city is flooded, this is regrettable; but the federal government does not have the obligation to make sure that no one ever undergoes economic hardship. We suggest, then, the governmental theory of paternalism—the government is going to take care of everybody for every reason. We suggest a disadvantage; it tends to make people too dependent on the state.

All right; second, we were told that the indigent often go without care rather than seek charity. Well, now that was an interesting assertion, ladies and gentlemen. I am going to ask you to search your memories and see if you have ever found any evidence presented on it. And after we have evidence, I'd like the gentlemen of the affirmative to quantify their problem. How many people don't seek *what* care for *what* reason?

Well, we were told, however, some of them do, you see, and this puts hospitals in trouble because the government doesn't pay sufficiently for the free patients which the hospitals accept. Now we're going to agree that the hospitals are in trouble. And we're going to suggest that the major fault of it belongs to the hospitals because, you see, they're inefficiently administered. James Brindle, the director of the Social Security Department of the United Auto Workers, said in the *Social Welfare Forum* for 1959, "Rapidly rising premiums are caused not only by justifiable improvements in hospital wage levels and working conditions and better technical facilities, but also by inadequate concern for the operating efficiency of hospitals, unwillingness to enforce legitimate controls, and a reluctance to experiment with new ideas." What is our point here, ladies and gentlemen? Simply this: The gentlemen of the affirmative say quite rightly that hospitals are in trouble; and then, instead of proposing to correct the problem, they propose to have the federal government step in and subsidize inefficiency and bad administration. We don't think that's an advantage; we think it is a distinct disadvantage. Indeed, Dr. Herman M. Somers, who is chairman of the Department of Political Science at Haverford College, told the National Council of Social Workers in May 1959 that the advocates of the affirmative resolution ". . . assume that if the government moved in they could continue present expensive and wasteful practices with assured payments, whereas now the countervailing pressure of organized consumers calling for more rigorous cost accounting and quality control appears to be growing steadily." Not only are the gentlemen of the affirmative subsidizing inefficiency; they are retarding the trends in the present system which will stop this inefficiency.

All right. Advantage number three: We're going to eliminate second-class citizenship. How? Well, we're going to make sure that the states no longer discriminate. It seems today that in some states people get good welfare care; in other states, they get bad welfare care and this is a distinct problem. All right, gentlemen, we agree with you; it's a problem, and we suggest, as the first affirmative perhaps anticipated we would, that there is a far more

106 simple answer to the problem than he's discussed with you. We simply pass a federal law, you see, standardizing state requirements for public assistance in medical care. It was done in social security; it was done in unemployment compensation; I see no reason why it couldn't be done under the present system. What's the disadvantage? Well, the gentlemen, by saying that the states are doing it today, admit that it is within the potential of the state to take care of the problem. They say, "Yes, the states can take care of the medically indigent; they're doing it today." The gentlemen of the affirmative just don't like the *way* they're doing it. Well, then, what you're doing is you're having the federal government assume a burden that the states can and are handling. We suggest a further centralization of our government, a further breakdown in the responsibility of the state, a further disadvantage of that resolution.

All right. Having viewed the advantages claimed for it, let's turn to the resolution itself. Well, you will recall we were told that, in the first place, a neglect of health today is causing death and suffering. I don't think anyone can dispute that the medical care of the American people is not what it should be. Nor do I think anyone can dispute that there has never been in the history of the world a nation whose medical standards were as high as they could be. In short, ladies and gentlemen, the medical needs of a people are always met less fully than they could be. What the gentlemen of the affirmative have to do in this debate is show you that the reason that these needs are not being met is economic and that their plan will take care of the need. Let's see whether this is true.

Well, first, we should ask ourselves how many people are there in the country affected by the need of the gentlemen of the affirmative? In other words, gentlemen, and we ask you directly, what percentage of the American people are not getting adequate medical care today because they can't afford to pay for it? Now we think that this is a very fair question. The entire need of the gentlemen is that there are people not getting care for financial reasons. Gentlemen, how many? How great is your need for a universal program? Now let's ask ourselves some additional questions. Well, first of all, if anyone in this country seeks medical care, is he prevented from getting it? Dr. Leonard Larson, who was then president of the American Medical Association and was later Chairman of the Medical Care Subcommittee of the White House Conference on the Aging, told the Senate Finance Committee in 1960, "We have proved again and again that no person in the United States need go without medical care because he is unable to pay for it." After an extensive study of the subject, the *Texas State Journal of Medicine* concluded in January 1959, "Evidence is lacking that any American, aged or otherwise, who has needed and actually sought health care has been denied it."

All right. Point one: No one is being denied care for financial reasons, but the gentlemen have told you people aren't getting adequate care and the negative agrees. Why is this? Well, we suggest the reasons are subjective in nature; they are not going to be cured by the resolution. For our authority, we'll turn to the most recent government statement on the problem, the *Background Paper on Health and Medical Care,* the White House Conference on the Aging, January 1961: "The reasons why people do or do not seek needed medical care are many. These in turn are often interrelated and complex, but they include such important factors as fear, habit, tradition, mores, religious belief, social dicta, degree of general education, degree of health education, and convenience of the service or facility for medical care." And in that whole long list—the most recent government statement on the problem, ladies and gentlemen—in that whole long list, I didn't hear the word *cost.* Let's ask ourselves more specifically, "Is cost a significant factor?" George Bugbee, president of the Health Information Foundation, *The Bulletin,* April 1959: "Economic factors seem to be a relatively minor element in this reluctance to see a physician." *National Survey of Old-Age and Survivors' Insurance Beneficiaries,* conducted again by the Department of Health, Education, and Welfare, 1957: "On the whole there appears but little systematic relationship between the amount of medical costs incurred by an elderly person and the amount of case income, or if he is married, the combined income of the couple."

All right. We suggest, then, three things: First, no one is denied care because he can't afford it; second, people are undermining their health primarily for subjective reasons that this resolution will not take care of; third, the economic factor is not determining in the question of medical care. Well, the gentlemen said, "Yes, but you see the problem"—the problem which we deny—"is inherent." Why? Well, first because no one can afford all the necessary insurance. Again, an assertion of the gentlemen introduced without evidence. Let's turn to Michael M. Davis, who was a member of various medical-care commissions set up by the government, who wrote in 1956 the book *National Health Insurance,* "Though the population covered by comprehensive plans is as yet only a few million, these plans have demonstrated that comprehensive high-quality medical care can be made available through health insurance at an annual cost of $150–$200 for a family." This is between 4 and 5 per cent of a family income of $4000. Perhaps this is the reason that Dr. Jerome B. Cohen of the City College of New York concluded in his 1958 book, *Decade of Decision,* "As comprehensive is now written under group plans, it is within the financial reach of even the most modest income employee." Well, we were told, yes, you see, but even after these people get insurance, it simply isn't enough. Why? Well, it doesn't cover all the cost. Now, gentlemen, we're going to accuse you of inadequate analysis here. We suggest that everyone in this room after debating the topic or listening to it this year knows there are five ways of paying medical care. You can take the money out of your pocket; you can borrow it from a bank; you can get it from private charity; you can get it from public charity; you can get it from voluntary insurance. Gentlemen, you have to show us that these five means taken *in toto,* taken together, taken as a unit, taken as a whole, if you will, are insufficient. Not just that one part is insufficient. Maybe that's why Marion Folsom, the former Secretary of Health, Education,

108 and Welfare, wrote in his pamphlet *Voluntary Health Insurance and Medical Care,* February 1958, "Of course, no one expects voluntary insurance arrangements to meet medical costs completely."

All right. The last question the negative will ask you in this debate: To what extent are these voluntary companies meeting their needs? Well, three surveys have been taken: Odin Anderson, 1957; Cornell University, 1956; Columbia University in 1959. They all reached the same conclusions. I'd like to quote from Dr. Anderson: "Studies which relate health insurance benefits to the medical expenses of insured persons indicate that some 75–94 per cent of all hospital expenses and 62–76 per cent of all surgical costs are covered."

Our conclusion: Those people who have insurance have their hospital bill covered up to 92 per cent, have their surgical bill covered up to 76 per cent. Insurance isn't supposed to do everything. You have to tell us that all the means taken *in toto* are inadequate, gentlemen, not just a fragmentary analysis presented for affirmative reasoning. We suggest, then, the rejection of the resolution stated. Thank you.

Second affirmative constructive speech: LAURENCE TRIBE.

Ladies and gentlemen, I felt a little strange clapping for what Frank has said because I'm afraid I can't agree with very much of it. I don't think that Frank really denied the basic contentions that Gene made in his first speech.

Let's go back, then, to that first speech and see what we tried to establish. We suggested to you that the neglect of health is today causing needless death and suffering in the United States, and it's important to note that the negative team admits that contention. We've got a third of a million unnecessary deaths every year; we have 400,000 contagious disease carriers receiving no medical treatment; we have half of all acute disabling medical conditions going untreated. All right. We suggested to you next that the primary reason for this neglect of health is that people are led to make medical decisions on economic grounds. And what did Frank say? Well, he said, number one, no one is denied needed medical care according to a very objective source, Dr. Larson of the American Medical Association. We're going to suggest that that's not responsive to our contentions; that whether or not anyone is denied care has nothing to do with whether people seek it for financial reasons, and we are going to suggest that, in addition to being irrelevant, Frank's statement is false. *The American Journal of Public Health* in May of 1960 says, "Incredible as it may seem in this enlightened century, we know only too well how tragically true and how increasingly frequent are the cases in which people are denied access to prescribed care because of their inability to pay." So we're going to suggest to you, in other words, that here is an increased additional advantage of the affirmative plan. People under the present system are indeed denied care because they can't pay for it; under compulsory health insurance they wouldn't be.

All right. The second point Frank made was that there are many reasons

for the neglect of health. They include fear, education, attitude, and so on,
and he seemed to make a great deal out of the fact that one publication he
very judiciously selected doesn't happen to mention cost. But, unfortunately,
we think that the problem cannot be dismissed in terms of lethargy or lack of
education or improper health attitudes. The former Assistant Secretary of the
Department of Health, Education, and Welfare, E. L. Richardson, wrote in
August of 1959, "We now have in America a citizenry that is keenly interested in health and that is generally aware of what is necessary and available
in medical care. The problem is not basically one of attitude or education,
but one of economics."

If the gentlemen are not going to discuss the authorities that we presented
so far, let's look further. Let's look to Professor J. Henry Richardson, writing
in *Economic and Financial Aspects of Social Security*, 1960. He says, "Illnesses
are often neglected in their early stages primarily because of the expenses
involved in medical care." The *New York Times*, December 7, 1959: "Millions
of Americans defer needed medical treatment primarily because of the fear of
cost." Professor Hazel Kyrk, *The Family in the American Economy*, 1953: "Field
studies have shown quantitatively that diagnosis and treatment are postponed or even foregone for economic reasons." That's why we concur with
the University of Michigan report to the Senate Finance Committee in June
of 1960, when they say that "income is the overwhelming determinant of
the ability to get needed medical care." That's why we agree with the Conference on the General Welfare, December 1959, when they say that the problem of health neglect in the United States is essentially economic.

We're not denying the existence of those other factors. We should move to
solve other problems, too, but the primary problem is one of cost and nothing that Frank said denied that.

All right, third of all, he turned to George Bugbee, again the president of a
voluntary agency, another objective source, telling us that there's no correlation between care and income and, therefore, that the economic factor is not
determining. We are going to challenge Mr. Bugbee's standards here. *The
Social Security Bulletin* of February 1961 says, "The latest national health
survey found that the amount of medical care received by a family was
significantly related to the family's income." We think that Mr. Bugbee is
just plain wrong and, furthermore, we don't think that any of the statements
that either Mr. Bugbee or Mr. Harrison made really refute any one of our three
points. You will recall, number one, we said many people just can't pay the
bills. Frank's response: "How many people?" Let's look again. Professor B. J.
Stern, *The Sociology of Medicine*, 1960. He says, "For the vast majority of the
people [and Gene read this in his first speech], adequate medical care is
simply beyond reach." We turn to Professor Stern, saying that this affects the
vast majority of the people. We turn to Professor Strauss, saying that the
result is a neglect of health. That wasn't really denied by the opposition. All
right. Then we suggested that even more people fear the ultimate cost even if
they can pay some of the bills. Frank had nothing to say on that point, and
the negative team refused to discuss with you our third point here and that

110   is that, even if you can pay all of the bills, all of us just tend to economize. We tend to economize because we may not feel sick enough to get care. And we think this constitutes in itself a very important reason for removing that dollar sign from medicine. Because, until we do, we've got a very important national problem of health neglect that we'd like to solve and that the negative team will do nothing about.

All right. The question then is: Is this problem of health neglect inherent in the present system? And Frank went through a rather rapid enumeration of the mechanisms of the present system — there were five of them — through which, somehow, you could pay for medical care. But you'll recall that we suggested to you that the reason the problem is inherent in the present system was, as Professor of Economics B. A. Weisbrod pointed out, that none of these mechanisms of the present system can remove the need to make economic decisions in seeking medical care. Most of those things that Frank said could be lumped under self-financing and here, of course, cost is directly a factor, and he didn't deny that proves, of course, the problem isn't solved here.

What about voluntary health insurance? We suggested to you that no one can afford all the insurance he needs, and this wasn't a matter of just assertion. We cited Professor Haverman saying that most people, as a result, decide to curtail their health insurance expenditure. The negative team couldn't deny that. What about the next point — that even if you decide to buy some kind of insurance, the amount you can buy depends upon how much money you have? The negative team distorted that to mean that insurance doesn't cover all the cost. That wasn't what we said at all, but now that the negative team has brought it up, what did Frank actually tell us? He said you could get comprehensive care for two hundred dollars a family. Now a little quick arithmetic shows you that if you multiply that by the number of families in the country, that means that this mythical company that's offering this policy would be collecting ten billion dollars' worth of premiums for twenty and a half billion dollars' worth of medical care! I think it would go out of business pretty fast. I'd like to see that policy. We don't think it's really comprehensive, and Professor Dickerson in his text on health insurance, 1960, corroborates that view. He says, "The Federal Trade Commission objects to the term 'comprehensive' in health insurance advertising. There simply is no comprehensive policy offered." And you know we've showed you that if you don't cover certain expenses, the economic decision in that area remains. So, we've got to have coverage. The negative team can't provide us that coverage; they can't even argue about the inherent defects of voluntary insurance. And, finally, they suggest, well, the problem isn't inherent because, well, perhaps, some people can get welfare.

And we suggested to you, number one, that welfare really isn't universal. You'll remember Gene said that the need was for a universal program because everyone is faced by economic decisions in seeking medical care, and, frankly, we don't know why the gentleman from Kings would restrict compulsory financed medical care only to the indigent. Number two, you'll recall that under that second advantage, Gene cited Edward Chase, and again it wasn't an assertion. Cited Edward Chase to the effect that a great many people are deterred from getting welfare by the stigma of the "means test," and here Frank said that there just isn't any evidence available on the subject. Well, the April 1961 *Report of the Iowa Department of Social Welfare* seems to think there is. They say there is no questioning the fact that a great many people have gone without needed medical care because they couldn't bring themselves to apply for this type of assistance through a welfare office. The report of the House Commerce Committee on March 10, 1954, concluded, "Economic means tests are in many areas serious barriers to hospital admission, threatening the public health through the perpetuation of serious infectious disease."

So, we think public welfare just isn't the adequate solution to our problems. We think it isn't universal; we think it's inadequate; we think there's a "means test" which deters people from getting care.

All right. What about the question of inadequate public welfare? This, you'll recall, was part of our third advantage, and Frank tried to relate that to the need by saying that perhaps by improving welfare we might be able to meet that need. Well, you'll remember that welfare doesn't allow people to decide whether or not to get medical care on the grounds of whether or not they need it. They've got to decide, first of all, whether or not they want to be degraded. But we'd like to suggest to you that Frank hasn't given us a workable counterplan for expanding welfare to the point where we could rely on it. In the Senate Finance Committee on June 29, 1960, Governor Nelson Rockefeller — and I suspect he knows something about financial matters — said that "The financing of state plans for expanded welfare will present serious financial strains on the states. It's likely that even with federal participation, a number of states couldn't participate at all." So we think that the negative's nebulous counterplan wouldn't meet the need; we don't think it's even related to the need because welfare doesn't remove the need to make decisions of economic origin in seeking medical care; and we're still left with a problem that the present system cannot meet.

That can be met by removing the question of how will the bill be paid, through a program of prepayment. Now what about those three advantages that would result from such a program? Number one: We suggested that we'd relieve economic insecurity, and Frank says, "Why is this the duty of the federal government?" We're not suggesting that it's the *duty* of the federal government; we're simply suggesting that it would be advantageous for the federal government to prevent medical tragedy from leading to financial disaster. And, frankly, I think the gentlemen from Kings are being a little inconsistent here. They advocate welfare to take care of people when they've already been forced into destitution, but they're not willing to prevent anyone from being forced into that welfare program.

All right. What about the second advantage that we'd prevent hospital insolvency? I think Frank misinterpreted this point and said we were talking something about higher premiums, and then suggested that we'd be subsi-

112   dizing inefficiency. I think that is a distortion. The fact is that more efficient administration of our hospitals is independent of the affirmative plan. We could accomplish it with or without the affirmative plan. The problem is those unpaid bills that are putting our hospitals out of business, and, as a matter of fact, Frank hasn't suggested any other way in which we could solve this very important need for some kind of action.

And that third area — that we'd remove medical inequality, that we'd provide adequate care to states that have inadequate care now for welfare services. Well, Frank says here there is a problem. What he'd have us do is standardize welfare levels. Presumably, since we showed you there aren't more funds in the states, he'd like to standardize them at the low levels of the present time. We don't think that's a solution. We think that again there's an undenied advantage to the affirmative plan here.

For these reasons, then, we still believe that we should remove the dollar sign from medicine — that we should adopt a program of compulsory health insurance for all citizens.

Second negative constructive speech: PETER SMITH.

Ladies and gentlemen, as second speaker for the negative in this debate, I'd like to go over the objections which we might have — which we *do* have — to the affirmative plan as it was suggested in the first affirmative speech, and then attempt to re-analyze some of the so-called affirmative advantages and attempt to look at them in a light a little bit more realistic than the gentlemen from Harvard have done.

First of all, in regard to that affirmative plan, we'd like to point out that, although we were given some very, very general details as to the cost and method of financing, we weren't told by the members of the affirmative team anything at all as to the general cost of their proposal. Now this, we think, is most interesting, because the members of the affirmative team, on one hand, are contending that the American people have a barrier of money between them and medical care which they need, and the whole philosophic basis of the affirmative case is this very interesting thesis: If we take the *dollar* sign out of medicine, we can solve the problem. And how are they going to take the dollar sign out of medicine? By that very old utopian method — we're going to let the government pay for the program and let the people take advantage of it, based upon their need. This is all very interesting. But I think, as even the gentlemen on my right must realize, that the government gets the money from *somewhere.* The government is going to collect this money from the very means which they suggested — some kind of compulsory tax. Now I'd like the members of the affirmative team to justify the fact that, on one hand, the American people don't have enough finances to pay for this system through the present method no matter what it might be; and yet on the other hand, somebody somewhere is going to have enough money so the federal government can get it in compulsory taxation and give it back to the hospitals and doctors, and provide the American people with free medical care. The illusion that one can remove the dollar sign from medicine is just that — an illusion — and the members of the affirmative team realize it. The only way in which that could be done is if doctors, hospitals, and all aspects of our medical facilities were to go completely without pay and give free service. The dollar sign isn't being removed; it's being transferred. We're going to have a middle man. And the members of the affirmative team cannot — at least, they haven't so far, and I don't think they can — say that it's going to be done at any greatly reduced cost.

First of all, according to the *Source Book of Health Insurance Data* for 1960, the total cost of medical care for the American people last year was approximately 18 billion dollars. Now, we'd like the members of the affirmative team to show us where the affirmative and where the federal government of their program is going to get this fund to finance the program. Secondly, we'd like the members of the affirmative team to justify one very important thing for us. We've been told on very general terms that the federal government is going to take over the entire system of financing medical care. By this we would presume that the federal government is going to pay everyone's medical bill for all of his medical expenses, and yet, throughout this debate (though we have been given some general philosophic needs and some general arguments as to some people who don't get medical care), there is nothing specific at all in this affirmative proposal. What do I mean by "specific"? Well, the members of the affirmative team not once have ever given us any reason why the federal government should pay the total medical bill. They haven't shown us that the American people experience any difficulty paying their dental expenses. They haven't shown us that we experience any difficulty paying our nonprescribed drug expenses. They haven't shown us that we experience any difficulty paying for sunglasses that doctors might prescribe. They haven't even shown us any particular reason where the need exists in the field of hospital care, surgical care, or personal-physician care. They have given us some general statements as to people who don't get the care. We'd like the members of the affirmative team to justify this particularly, so they can prove to us we should allow the federal government to take over the entire system. Granted (and we will grant this for about ten seconds) there may be a need in some specific area, but we'd like the members of the affirmative team to show us that it exists in every facet of our medical system today, because this is the only ground upon which they could justify a plan which supposedly pays everyone's medical bills. The plan, it seems, is about X times larger than the affirmative need. I had to say "X" because I don't know exactly how big the affirmative need is.

But, again, the members of the affirmative team should show us exactly why there's a need for the federal government to pay the full amount of everyone's medical bill. Well, then the members of the affirmative team went a little bit further. They told us that they're going to have local boards to regulate any abuses which might creep into the system. This is all well and good; the affirmative team is suspecting that there are going to be some

114   abuses. But we contend that local boards aren't a satisfactory means of solving the problem. My colleague pointed out that the hospitals are in a financial mess due to the present system. I can read some quotations here pointing out that, in many cases, there are abuses on the local level. Either some doctors who don't live up to the code they're supposed to live up to, or many patients who want to take advantage of a free system, or many hospital administrators and persons in hospitals, either through negligence or through crookedness, will take advantage of such a type of proposal.

Now the members of the affirmative team have provided for some type of regulation, but it's on a local and not a federal or even state level. In other words, the very persons who, under the present system (and under their proposal also) may perpetrate the violations, are going to be judges in their own cases under the affirmative proposal. This too will add to the general cost — the X cost of that affirmative proposal — a significant disadvantage of the affirmative team.

Well, in regard to the so-called overall points given to us by the members of the affirmative team in this debate in regard to advantages, we were told there are three things wrong with the present system. Now these things aren't needs in the debater's sense — they're needs as far as the United States is concerned. And the affirmative proposal, it just happens, is going to solve these needs. Now it's the contention of the members of the negative team that, first of all, the affirmative proposal won't solve these problems, and, secondly, it's going to make some of them a great deal worse than they are under the present system.

You'll recall one of them is the contention by the members of the affirmative team that we're going to remove the financial drain of free care on the hospitals. Well, my colleague pointed out that they weren't giving you the whole story there, that a great part of the reason why hospitals are in financial difficulties is through their own inefficiency — through practices, and *bad* practices, which occur in the hospitals. What was the answer of the second affirmative speaker to this point? He told you, well, first of all, we're going to get rid of the free care which hospitals have to give, and, secondly, we didn't propose any alternative. Now we don't think it's the obligation of the members of the negative team to provide a counterplan. We'd only like to point out that, first of all, this affirmative proposal won't specifically be solving the whole problem, since a great part of the problem is hospital inefficiency and they are taking no federal or state means to solve the problem of hospital inefficiency. Secondly, the members of the affirmative team have, more or less, by asking us to provide a solution, admitted that the problem exists within the present system.

But let's carry it one step further. We don't think it's just a problem of hospitals being run wrong or hospitals having to give a lot of free care to people who can't afford to pay their bills. We think it's something which goes much deeper, for there is a general shortage of hospital and general medical facilities throughout the United States, and it's the contention of the members of the negative team that the affirmative proposal won't come anywhere near to solving this problem. Now why is this so? Well, I made a big point out of the lack of substantial and adequate regulation before. Why did I do this? Well, I did this because it's one of the things that comes about when you have a complete—and nothing could be more complete than this affirmative proposal—a complete system of prepayment for medical expenses. F. J. Snyder, a research analyst for the Public Affairs Institute, *Health Insurance for the Aged*, 1960: "An unfortunate by-product of the increased use of hospitalization insurance is the over-utilization of hospital facilities. The abuse of medical insurance results in further packing already overloaded hospitals." And Mr. Snyder concludes his statement by saying, "Any successful government-sponsored health insurance will have to meet the problem of *unnecessary* use of hospitals and *unnecessary* surgery."

I stress the word "unnecessary" because I realize the affirmative are quite willing to come up here and say that this increased use of hospitals will be for the people who aren't getting the care now. I say "unnecessary" because it will be persons who don't need medical care and yet who will flock to these hospitals and to these doctors and overutilize these facilities. And there is very definitely a shortage. I don't think I have to prove it, but I'd like to point out exactly how seriously it exists and where it exists. *U.S. News and World Report*, May 9, 1958: "Because of the short supply of doctors, hospitals often cannot obtain the physicians they need even when they seek to hire them."

Now the members of the affirmative team may well try to point out that their program—their program of X amount of compulsory health insurance—is going to solve this problem, this problem of hospitals being abused, this problem of an overutilization of facilities or a shortage of doctors, but it just isn't so. Professors Baisden and Hutchinson, the University of California, *Health Insurance*, 1958: "The mere act of providing more money for medical care does not necessarily result in an increase in either the quantity or quality of services." Mr. F. J. Follman, Jr., a director of the Research and Information Bureau of the Health Insurance Association of America, *Voluntary Health Insurance and Medical Care*, 1958: "The existence of a broadly established insurance mechanism, no matter how effective, does not, nor can it, increase the medical personnel or facilities available."

What conclusion can we reach here? One of the advantages that we're supposedly going to have when we adopt this affirmative proposal is the fact that medical care is going to be made more adequate. Everyone's going to have the wonderful advantages of adequate medical care just due to the adoption of this affirmative proposal. But we pointed out that we do have a problem of a shortage of facilities and doctors. The affirmative has no adequate measures in its plan for providing against unnecessary over-utilization of these facilities, and compulsory health insurance *per se* won't solve this problem, and what's going to be the result? Well, Mr. Seely Greenberg, a medical reporter for the Providence *Journal*, in *Harper's*, October 1960: "The frequent instances of careless medical care given by overworked doctors are among the most frequent complaints of patients today." In other words, we

116 can see that overworked doctors, overstrained facilities, give inadequate medical care. And the affirmative proposal is going to worsen this situation, leading to a greater amount of inadequacy in medical care given to the American people. They aren't meeting the advantage; they're creating an even greater disadvantage through the adoption of the affirmative proposal.

For these reasons and the objections to the need which my colleague brought up before, and which he will continue in the first negative rebuttal, we beg that the affirmative proposal be rejected. Thank you.

First negative rebuttal speech: FRANK HARRISON.

Ladies and gentlemen, as first speaker for the negative, returning to this podium, I'd like to discuss with you again the question of whether or not there's a need for the affirmative resolution, and I'd like to discuss with you some of the refutations of arguments which the second affirmative speaker wishes I'd made.

Now the first thing you'll recall that I asked the affirmative team was, "Specifically, gentlemen, how many people in the United States are not getting adequate medical care because they can't afford to pay for it?" I said, "Gentlemen, give us the statistics." And that was a very clever answer we heard. We were told, according to some authority, that the vast majority of the American people can't afford on their own resources to pay for medical care, and that simply does not answer the question. The question, gentlemen, to repeat, is, "How many people aren't getting care because they can't afford to pay for it?" Perhaps the vast majority can't afford it on their own resources — but you'll recall there are five ways in which they can pay for medical care, only one of which is straight out of their own resources. They can borrow; they can go to charity; they can have insurance; but, simply, the answer given does not reply to the question.

Well, then we were told, you see, that people are making medical decisions on economic grounds. I came to the rostrum and I quoted Dr. Larson, who was not very objective, I'm sorry; he was testifying under oath at the time, however. But some authority, however — and I think this is cute — some authority knows the circumstances in which people are denied care because they can't afford it. I wish that authority would tell the American Hospital Association, because their president appeared before the House Ways and Means Committee, in July of 1959, and he said, "I am not aware of cases where people have been refused hospital and medical service because of their inability to pay for it." And, furthermore, a representative of the AFL-CIO, Mr. Cruikshank, was asked the now-famous debater's question by Congressman Alger of Texas, to please give examples of the circumstances — give specific cases in which people have been denied care — and I think the gentlemen can search the record of the House Committee on Ways and Means and will find that Mr. Cruikshank notably did not reply. All right, we went on a little further. You'll recall I quoted from the most recent source I could get hold of, the White House Conference in January 1961. They said there were many reasons why people aren't getting care. The gentlemen said, "Well, it was nice of the negative team to pick out the one source that would go along with them." It was also nice for the negative team that that source happened to be the most recent and the most authoritative. But they said, "Well, you see, there are a lot of other problems involved here; we admit this. The problem is that economics is the main problem." Now, gentlemen, even if we concede that for a minute, you're missing the point. The point is your need isn't going to meet your plan because you've admitted that there are other barriers besides economic barriers; so even assuming this grand hypothesis, even assuming that we're going to be able to strike down the financial barrier, the other barriers still remain. The other barriers are still effective. People still aren't going to doctors, and that very lovely need isn't met by that comprehensive plan.

Well, we were told, "Yes, you see, but income is the overwhelming determinant." All right, ladies and gentlemen, I'd like to take a look at what happens when that overwhelming determinant is taken away. Drs. Odin Anderson and Paul Shipley, *Comprehensive Medical Insurance*, 1959. They begin by discussing the fact that there are three plans—the General Health Insurance Plan, the Health Insurance Plan of New York, and the Windsor Insurance Plan—which prepay the patient's visit to the doctor's office in the first place. They pay for the patient every time he goes to the doctor's office. Obviously, no cost to him.

Now according to the theory of this affirmative team, wouldn't you think that people would be going to doctors far more frequently than they are when they don't have such insurance? Let's look at the conclusions. A recent release of the *National Health Survey* showed that 37 per cent of the population had not seen a physician within a year. Under the most favorable financial circumstances, the absence of any such barriers to physician services in G.H.I., H.I.P., and Windsor, 25–32 per cent of the enrollees will not seek physicians' services within a year; 37 per cent don't go when they don't have insurance; 32 per cent don't go when they *do* have insurance. Gentlemen, we suggest your economic determinant isn't determining too much.

Well, then, we were told, you see, that all the negative sources in the debate simply don't stand because Mr. Bugbee, Mr. Bugbee is the president of an insurance company. Now I'm a little tired of hearing Mr. Bugbee assailed for bias in this debate. He happens to be President of the Health Information Foundation, which is not employed by the insurance companies. And even if he is, we suggest that the Department of Health, Education, and Welfare has not yet come under the pay of the insurance companies and I cited them, too, and the gentlemen never replied.

Well, then you'll recall I said there are five ways of paying for medical care. I said the gentlemen had to indict each one of them, and I ask you to search your memories to see if they have; they haven't indicted government payments, they haven't indicted private charity, they haven't indicted ability to borrow. They said, "No, gentlemen, you don't get the point. The point is that these don't remove the necessity for economic decisions." Gentlemen, you

118   haven't shown us what evils are following from these economic decisions; you haven't even shown us that they're leading to concrete harm, but there are three advantages to the affirmative resolution. The first one, you see, is it's going to prevent hardship. Now I suggested to the gentlemen that it's not the duty of the government to prevent people from going into debt to any degree. The gentlemen said, "Oh, that isn't the problem; they're going to become destitute under the present system." Gentlemen, would you present some statistics to prove that a significant number of people are becoming destitute? Also, we suggested that it's going to create a paternalistic welfare state. No comment from the gentlemen. Well, then we were told that the indigent go without care. I said, "Very interesting, in fact. Indigent go without care rather than seek it." And according to the second affirmative speaker, I said there was no evidence available. No! I said the second affirmative had to tell us how many people in the indigent group don't get care because they can't afford it, and we still haven't heard that answer. But we were told, you see, that the more efficient administration of hospitals will occur independent of the resolution. I read an authority in this debate, Dr. Somers, that said it wouldn't. That it would occur under the present system and not the resolution. I think we can conclude that the resolution still deserves to be rejected. Thank you.

First affirmative rebuttal speech: LAURENCE TRIBE.

After fifteen minutes of negative optimistic discussion about what the gentlemen of the opposition consider "a very lovely need," we're led to believe that perhaps there is no real problem at all—that perhaps it's just some wild rumor started by 400,000 contagious disease carriers. We're going to resist the temptation to reach that conclusion because there are a couple of objections that we've got to cover before we can go back and see why that conclusion is fallacious.

Now, the gentlemen asked us, "How much will the plan cost?" They were very concerned about that fact. We turn to Dr. Alan Gregg in *Challenges to Contemporary Medicine,* 1957. He says that by spending only 6 per cent more than we currently spend on medical care, the government, through compulsory national health insurance, could provide completely comprehensive medical services for everyone. By using the gentlemen's own figure of 18 billion dollars, that means that we'd spend about 1.08 billion dollars more than we currently spend on medical care. Frankly, we think that the needless death and suffering in the present system really is worth about one billion dollars at least.

Now the gentlemen say that actually there is some big problem here because we couldn't get enough money under the affirmative plan because you haven't got enough money now. Well, number one, we weren't talking only about the inadequacy of funds; we were talking about decisions. Number two, people pay taxes progressively; they don't pay medical bills progressively. Then the gentlemen said, "Where is the money going to come from?" Well, it's going to come from income taxes. In *Public Finance*, 1960, Professor Troy Cauley points out, "Because of the interrelationship between government spending and the economy, far higher tax levels would in no way impair our economic growth." Then the gentlemen suggested that there were all kinds of things like dental expenditures and drug expenses, and sunglasses, I suppose, that we ought to have discussed very specifically. Well, frankly, I thought Gene covered quite a bit in that first ten minutes without trying to apply all of his arguments to every one of these areas. We think the area of dental care is perhaps typical. *Public Health Reports,* March '59, says, "Only 31 per cent of the American people who seriously need dental work are getting it at the present time, primarily because of the high cost involved." So, frankly, we think that our need really does apply to all of these areas.

They told us that local boards are unsatisfactory. We've got 430 of them working pretty satisfactorily now. They said overutilization would result. Well, number one, that contradicts their idea that there's no cost barrier; number two, it could be effectively controlled. *The Evaluation of Medical Care Programs,* 1961, points out, "It's been shown empirically that unnecessary or wasteful use of medical services can be effectively controlled with no adverse consequences." They suggested that doctors would be setting their own fees; they forget that doctors and laymen sit on those boards. They told us that there were going to be abuses, and yet James Brindle in the *American Journal of Public Health,* April '57, says, "Services must be completely prepaid if the economic barrier to needed care is to be removed, and if unnecessary surgery or hospitalization is to be discouraged." That shows the need for comprehensive care, doesn't it?—not the reason for rejecting the affirmative plan.

Finally, they suggested we've got too few facilities now. Number one, we say that even if we've got fewer facilities than we would like to have, that's no reason to determine who gets to use those facilities on the basis of who's the highest bidder. Number two, we say we don't really have a serious facility problem. *The New York State Medical Journal* on May 15, 1959, said, "If the public fully utilized the preventive, diagnostic, and treatment services and facilities already available, a great many of the illnesses now fatal could be effectively treated." So let's look back at some of those illnesses; let's see what the primary reason for the neglect of health is in the United States today. Now, number one, it was suggested that no one is denied care. And we're told, finally, that it's really true because Dr. Larson was under oath. Well, frankly, we still think that the *American Journal of Public Health* really wasn't speaking purely out of its imagination when it suggested that people are denied care. The issue was peripheral to the direct question, but we still think it constitutes an advantage of the affirmative proposal. But the question wasn't "Who is denied?"—the question is, "Why don't people seek that care?" And we presented Professor Richardson, Professor Kyrk, the University of Michigan report, and the Conference on the General Welfare, all saying that the primary reason that they didn't seek that care was economic. The gentlemen come back and tell us that the economic factor isn't deter-

120 mining because there's no real correlation between money and medicine in the United States, and they say the Department of Health, Education, and Welfare agrees with them. And that the Department of Health, Education, and Welfare National Health Survey for last year concluded that utilization rates go up 23 per cent as income goes down 25 per cent. So we're going to suggest to you that there really is a very basic problem in all of these areas; that when the affirmative team asks us what happens when the economic factors are removed, they'd know what we have already shown you—and that is that when the economic factors are removed (as they were removed in the case of Georgia, for instance, according to the American Medical Association in 1954), millions of people get that care who hadn't gotten it before. In that particular instance, one million three hundred and eighty thousand people, when screening surveys were offered on an experimental basis, received free medical care that they hadn't gotten before the cost barrier had been removed. That's what happens. Cost is the major factor, not education.

All right, what about the question of the inherency within the present system? The gentlemen first suggested that comprehensive policies could be given to all of us for $200. When they saw the absurdity of that suggestion, they dropped it completely in this debate. They no longer contend that they can provide that kind of policy. They have nothing left here really, because they're not denying, number one, that the economic decision remains when you've got to decide whether or not to buy voluntary health insurance; they're not denying, number two, that the amount you can buy depends on how much money you have. They're not denying that in welfare or in any free program, people are deterred by the "means test," so it doesn't free people to make medical decisions on medical grounds. And they're not denying, finally, that if we adopted that affirmative plan we could prevent a great deal of economic hardship; we could improve our welfare program; we could prevent our hospitals from going broke as a result of unpaid bills. All they say is that there still will be other problems that your program may not solve. We don't think that's a reason to reject our plan. We think we still should remove the dollar sign from medicine.

Second negative rebuttal speech: PETER SMITH.

Ladies and gentlemen, as last speaker for the negative, I'd like to summarize the debate for the final time this week end. First of all, the objections which I raised to the affirmative plan were answered rather hastily by the first affirmative rebuttalist. We were told that some expert says that we can finance the entire program at a cost of only 6 per cent greater than the present system, and this is something that our economy can bear; so, therefore, there's no real problem. Now, gentlemen, I think anyone associated with this debate topic knows that I could bring up ten sources saying your administrative cost would be 6, 12, 8, 15, even 18 per cent; just as you brought up one saying it was 6 per cent. But the essential question that I asked was: Are you supposedly going to remove the dollar sign from the area of financing medical care? At least that was the basic affirmative thesis in this debate. Yet I pointed out in my second negative speech that you aren't really doing this at all. All you're doing is transferring it, so that the federal government takes the money from the citizens of America to provide their medical care, instead of the people paying it directly, or indirectly through various facets of the present system. You aren't really removing the dollar sign. It is still going to be a cost for the American people to bear, of financing their medical care. Now, according to your statements, the present system is too much for the American people to bear. I asked you to break it down and consider it separately so I wouldn't have to do what I'm about to do. But you wouldn't do it so far, so I will.

The only estimate we have so far of just what the affirmative proposal is going to entail is the fact that it's going to pay everyone's expenses for every type of medical care. This is fine. The present system — everything — costs 18 billion dollars. Theirs is going to cost 6 per cent more, and yet the American people, according to the entire affirmative stand upon this floor, can't afford the present system in its totality. So, therefore, we think the members of the affirmative team have pulled one of the greatest illogical conclusions of all time. They are contending the American people can't afford a system, and in order to help them pay their way out of this problem, we're going to provide them with a system which is going to take more money from them, remove the dollar sign from the area of medical economics, and make everybody happy. Gentlemen, this is Utopia, this is Utopia carried to its furthest extreme. Again, an example of where the affirmative proposal does not show too much of a demonstration of its correlation to the affirmative needs.

Well, then, we pointed out that regulation by local boards would be deficient. They said doctors and laymen will sit on the board. This doesn't prove again that you're going to stop all kinds of abuses which exist at various levels. My colleague pointed out that the reason why hospitals are in trouble is because hospitals have inefficient practices. No real answer here given by the members of the affirmative team. The affirmative proposal of compulsory health insurance is going to make this problem worse. As far as overutilization of facilities is concerned, the affirmative team "whitewashed" it. I pointed out that one of the things they're going to do — one of the needs they're supposed to solve — is the adequacy of American medical care. And the result of this unnecessary overutilization of facilities is going to be a decrease in the adequacy of medical care made available to the American people. The members of the affirmative team had no answer here; an advantage turned into a distinct disadvantage.

Now in regard to the affirmative need. Now, I have no intention of running here through every single quote fired at you by the first affirmative speaker and fired right back by my colleague, and then refired by the members of the affirmative team, but I think one thing stands clear. First of all, despite the fact that a great many people die in the United States every year, it hasn't been established by the members of the affirmative team that these people die because they couldn't get needed medical care, because they

122   couldn't afford the treatment, and this is the only logical basis on which we should adopt the affirmative proposal. And the reason why is very simple—because my colleague has contended throughout this debate that there are other factors besides purely economic ones which keep people from seeking needed medical care—everything from negligence to pure ignorance. The members of the affirmative team at first flirted with the idea of completely refuting this. When we came to the first affirmative rebuttal, they were accepting it. They were saying, "But the primary reason is economic." Primary or not, my colleague matched the first affirmative speaker source for source, saying that you won't solve the problem by giving the people the money to go to the doctor, and he gave the specific example of where it's been done, the utilization of services didn't increase one bit. In other words, we can see that the affirmative proposal won't get at the heart of the problem—making the American people get adequate medical care when they have the means available to them.

Well, the members of the affirmative team move a little bit further. They indict the so-called present system by considering voluntary health insurance, and they tell us that just because the amount of voluntary health insurance you have depends upon the amount of money you have, there's something wrong with voluntary health insurance. Well, my colleague pointed out the other facets of the present system. Most of them were completely ignored by the members of the affirmative team. They go back constantly to their basic thesis, that we've got to take financial problems out of the area of medicine in the United States today. Now this we don't think is the obligation of the federal government. It certainly isn't being very well handled by the members of the affirmative team for this very simple reason: The federal government, or the United States as a political body, has no obligation to make sure that everyone in the United States gets lavish special care or has all his economic problems solved. This would be quite a job for the federal government. But the federal government does have some kind of obligation to make sure that the American people get medical care when they need it, and this has no bearing upon the members of the affirmative team's contention that the fact that the American people—some of them—die when they don't get adequate medical care. The affirmative in this debate haven't established an essential specific reason for adopting this resolution, and the second affirmative speaker in his rebuttal must show you that, first of all, their specific plan *per se* will solve the evil that they say exists in its totality, or else the affirmative proposal won't meet that evil. The need can be solved by other means, and we need not adopt that resolution. Thank you.

Second affirmative rebuttal speech: GENE CLEMENTS.

Before we return to the need, let's look again at the few objections which the negative managed to sustain after Larry refuted them. They brought back the idea that we were just transferring the dollar sign. Now, granted we are transferring *a* dollar sign, but the crucial thing is that we're transferring it from the individual, where it deters care, to the government. Where the government pays it from a progressive tax, the individual no longer has to make an individual economic decision every time he wants care. And we've shown you, I believe, that that individual economic decision is the main cause for health neglect. That, we contend, is wherein we are transferring the dollar sign. And the gentlemen ask us how in the world we can possibly pay for it if we contend we can't pay for it now. Again they mistake the fact that we're doing it on an individual basis. We say there are many who can't pay for care. All of us are deterred. However, through a progressive tax we can let everyone's care be paid for because, of course, the individual no longer has to meet all of his expenses if he is low income — if, indeed, he can't pay for his care. We certainly wouldn't think that the gentlemen of the negative are contending that this nation is too poor, too cheap, to provide adequate care to all its citizens. So we think that these objections to the affirmative proposal certainly don't stand.

Let's go back to the need itself. In the first area, we said there was a neglect of health which led to needless death and suffering. For a while this was admitted; then the gentlemen wanted to know if these people died because they couldn't afford care. Well, my colleague directly related the one third of a million who die needlessly (that's one out of every five deaths each year) to essentially economic problems. In the area of, for instance, one half of all disabling acute illnesses, we sort of assumed that it was apparent that if these people are flat on their backs, they know they need care. There must be a pretty good reason why they're not getting that care. We suggested that that factor was the economic factor. And I think we proved it when we gave you Professor Richardson, the *New York Times*, Professor Kyrk, the University of Michigan survey, all of which concluded that income was the overwhelming determinant. But the gentlemen say, no, there are other factors. Certainly there are other factors, gentlemen; we never contended there weren't. We gave you testimony that these factors were relatively insignificant, which as yet has gone undenied. We showed you surveys in Georgia, for instance, where over a million people came out to get free preventive examinations. Eighty-five per cent of those people had not been diagnosed previously.

Let's go a little bit further, however; let's go to Philadelphia, where the A.F. of L. Medical Center in Philadelphia provides preventive examinations for certain union members at no cost. A survey recently conducted revealed that, were it not for this free center, 92 per cent of the members receiving preventive care would never have sought diagnosis. It suggests to us that indeed there may be a cost barrier to medical care, a cost barrier which in fact transcends those who simply can't afford care, and encompasses all of us, and this is the point which the negative has never refuted. The idea that it's not the cost of care alone, but the fact that we must make an economic decision in seeking that care, which extends the need to everyone of us in this room. Everyone of us, every time we put off a physical examination because we want to economize (we want to save the ten, fifteen, twenty dollars it costs for a physical examination), has made an economic decision

124 which has harmed our health. We contend that compulsory health insurance can remove the need to make those economic decisions. *Public Medical Care,* by Dr. Franz Goldman, pointed out, "By providing easy access to early diagnosis and thorough treatment, compulsory health insurance would greatly reduce the frequency of serious stages of illness." Compulsory health insurance can certainly meet the need in this particular area.

The gentlemen introduced the peripheral idea that people aren't denied care. Well, of course, this isn't particularly relevant to our case. We're worried about the people who never seek care in the first place. But, indeed, people *are* denied care. Hearings of the House Ways and Means Committee: "There is ample evidence, documented by studies in Michigan, in Boston, in California, and throughout the nation, that because of inability to pay for it, literally millions of Americans go without needed medical care." So very definitely there is a problem in this area, and certainly we feel that the removal of the need to make those economic decisions can solve the problem. We showed you in the area of inherency that voluntary insurance — and basically, all these so-called other five factors could be lumped as either voluntary insurance, welfare, or self-financing — voluntary insurance could not remove the need to make economic decisions. In fact, it depended upon the income of the individual purchasing the insurance. And the negative never responded to either of these ideas. They presented a comprehensive policy which proposed for ten billion dollars to give twenty billion dollars' worth of care. When we pointed out the absurdity of that, they dropped the point. We showed you in welfare that the "means test" deterred care — in fact, that welfare was inadequate; we shouldn't expand welfare. And in this particular area, again, the negative has dropped their point.

Ladies and gentlemen, the opposition, and, indeed, all of us here, the gentlemen have made cost a primary consideration. They ask us how we'll pay the bill. We've shown you that we can pay the cost of the affirmative proposal in dollars and cents. The negative proposal is today being paid for through human death and suffering. How, gentlemen, will *you* pay the bill?

Angle, Paul M., ed. *Created Equal?* Chicago: The University of Chicago Press, 1958. For the complete Lincoln-Douglas Debates of 1858.

Kraus, Sidney, ed. *The Great Debates*. Bloomington: Indiana University Press, 1962. For the Kennedy-Nixon television debates of 1960.

McBath, James H., ed. *T.V. Championship Debates*. Portland, Me.: J. Weston Walch, Publishers, 1964. For intercollegiate debates on television.

Mills, Glen E. *Reason in Controversy*. Boston: Allyn and Bacon, Inc., 1964. For the Lodge-Boothby Debate in 1961 on the admission of Red China to the United Nations.

Nichols, Egbert Ray, ed. *Intercollegiate Debates*. New York: Noble and Noble, Publishers, Inc., 1919 –.

Printed transcripts of the championship rounds of debate at West Point beginning with the 1964 debate are available without charge. Request the *Report of Results* for a specific year by writing to Director, National Debate Tournament, United States Military Academy, West Point, New York 10996.

Taped recordings of the championship rounds of debate at West Point are available without charge. Send a blank 1800-foot reel to Signal Officer, United States Military Academy, West Point, New York 10996, ATTN: Recording Studio. The debate will be transcribed on the blank reel and returned to the sender.

University Debater's Annual. New York: H. W. Wilson Company, 1914 –.

Webster, Daniel. *Reply to Hayne,* ed. by Cornelius Beach Bradley. Boston: Allyn and Bacon, 1918.

Windes, Russel R., and Arthur N. Kruger, eds. *Championship Debating*. Portland, Me.: J. Weston Walch, Publishers, 1961. For selected final rounds of the West Point debates.

The following list of books and the chart are provided for the convenience of (1) those who will use *Fundamentals of Debate: Theory and Practice* as the core textbook but will occasionally want more material on a particular subject, or (2) those who will use one of the listed books as the core textbook and *Fundamentals of Debate: Theory and Practice* as a supplementary textbook. Cross-references to the following books are provided on the chart:

Capp, Glenn R., and Thelma Robuck Capp. *Principles of Argumentation and Debate*. Englewood Cliffs, N.J., 1965.

Ehninger, Douglas, and Wayne Brockriede. *Decision by Debate*. New York, 1963.

Ewbank, Henry Lee, and J. Jeffery Auer. *Discussion and Debate*, 2nd ed. New York, 1951.

Freeley, Austin J. *Argumentation and Debate*. San Francisco, 1961.

Huber, Robert B. *Influencing Through Argument*. New York, 1963.

Kruger, Arthur N. *Modern Debate: Its Logic and Strategy*. New York, 1960.

McBath, James H., ed. *Argumentation and Debate: Principles and Practices*, rev. ed. New York, 1963.

McBurney, James H., and Glen E. Mills. *Argumentation and Debate: Techniques of a Free Society*, 2nd ed. New York, 1964.

Mills, Glen E. *Reason in Controversy*. Boston, 1964.

	Ch. 1	Ch. 2	Ch. 3	Ch. 4	Ch. 5	Ch. 6	Ch. 7
Capp & Capp	3,4,6	10	3,10	5,7-9	11	12,13	
Ehninger & Brockriede	7,14	15	15	4-6, 8-11	12,16	17,18, 20	21
Ewbank & Auer	6,10, 11	25	25	5,7,8	9,27	24,26	28
Freeley	2,3	14	15	4,5,7, 8	6,7,10, 16	17,19 20,23	21
Huber	2,3	11,12	11,12	4-9	5-10	13,14	
Kruger	2,3	4,5,7	4,5,7	6,10- 13,15	8,10- 17	18,19, 24	22
McBath	2,4	6,7	6,7	5,9, 10	11	12-14	17
McBurney & Mills	1-4	12,13	12,13	5-10	7,8,16, 17	14,15, 19	19
Mills	2-4	9	9	5-7	6,7,10	10,11	

Chapter 1, p. 12.

1. Resolved: That the Communist Party should be outlawed in the United States.
2. Proposition of policy
3. Harold E. Stassen
4. Thomas E. Dewey
5. There are five issues, the first of which is admitted:
   a. Are Communist organizations a threat to the United States and to World Peace?
   b. Are present laws inadequate to meet the Communist threat?
   c. Would outlawing the Communist Party be an effective means of controlling the Communist threat?
   d. Would the Mundt-Nixon bill outlaw the Communist Party?
   e. Would outlawing the Communist Party be a violation of our Constitutional liberties?
6. A prima facie case was not presented. Two of the issues were not considered sufficiently by Stassen. Present laws were virtually ignored; he simply made the statement that we had no law to effectively control the Communist threat. Also, Stassen did not demonstrate that outlawing the Communist Party would be an effective means of controlling the threat. Whether the Mundt-Nixon bill would actually outlaw the Communist Party was largely a matter of interpretation.

Chapter 2, p. 29.

Resolved: __4__
I. __7__
   A. __16__
      1. __14__
      2. __6__
   B. __11__
      1. __2__
      2. __10__
II. __3__
   A. __12__
   B. __8__
III. __9__
   A. __15__
   B. __1__
   C. __13__
   D. __5__

Chapter 3, p. 42.

Resolved: __3__
I. __10__
   A. __6__
      1. __4__
      2. __12__
   B. __14__
      1. __11__
      2. __7__
II. __8__
   A. __2__
   B. __13__
III. __5__
   A. __9__
   B. __1__

Chapter 4, p. 57.   *Chapter 5, p. 71.*

1. Analogy (figurative)	Stevenson	Eisenhower
2. Sign	1. A	2. I
3. Cause	3. C	4. L
4. Example	5. E	6. O
5. Sign	7. D	8. K
6. Cause	9. F	10. J
7. Analogy (literal)	11. H	12. P
8. Example	13. B	14. M
	15. G	16. N

Chapter 6, p. 86.

Resolved: That the selective service policies of the United States should be re-examined.

I. There is a need for a change, for
  A. Our military system is inefficient and costly, for
      1. About 750,000 men, some of high quality, will leave the armed forces in 1956, and
      2. The government will spend $2,500,000,000 for the basic training of replacements alone.
  B. The draft is not meeting our military needs, for
      1. It doesn't supply the experienced personnel needed for modern weapons, and
      2. It doesn't provide the incentives for quality men to make the service a career.
II. The affirmative proposes the following plan:
  A. Strengthen the incentives for a military career, and
  B. End the draft as soon as it is consistent with national security.
III. Significant benefits will result from the affirmative plan, for
  A. Our armed forces would be strengthened, for
      1. Experienced and professional personnel would be retained in the military.
  B. We could meet our needs on a voluntary basis.

Chapter 7, p. 99.

1. L
2. P
3. P
4. P
5. L
6. P
7. L
8. P